Shantyboat
ON THE *Bayous*

Shantyboat ON THE *Bayous*

HARLAN HUBBARD

with illustrations by the author
and a Foreword by Don Wallis

THE UNIVERSITY PRESS OF KENTUCKY

Drawings and prints by Harlan Hubbard and photographs from
his collection are reproduced through the courtesy of Bill
Caddell, Paul Hasfurder, and Don Wallis.

Copyright © 1990 by The University Press of Kentucky

Scholarly publisher for the Commonwealth,
serving Bellarmine College, Berea College, Centre
College of Kentucky, Eastern Kentucky University,
The Filson Club, Georgetown College, Kentucky
Historical Society, Kentucky State University,
Morehead State University, Murray State University,
Northern Kentucky University, Transylvania University,
University of Kentucky, University of Louisville,
and Western Kentucky University.

Editorial and Sales Offices: Lexington, Kentucky 40506-0336

Library of Congress Cataloging-in-Publication Data
Hubbard, Harlan.
  Shantyboat on the bayous / Harlan Hubbard ; with illustrations by
the author and a foreword by Don Wallis.
    p. cm.
  ISBN 0-8131-1717-8 :
  1. New Orleans Region (La.)—Description and travel. 2. Bayous—
Louisiana. 3. Louisiana—Description and travel—1951-1980.
4. Hubbard, Harlan—Journeys—Louisiana—New Orleans Region.
5. Shantyboats and shantyboaters—Louisiana—New Orleans Region.
I. Title.
F379.N54H83 1990
917.63'350463—dc20   89-77898

This book is printed on acid-free paper meeting
the requirements of the American National Standard
for Permanence of Paper for Printed Library Materials.

Foreword

"I still cherish my longing for a new life," Harlan Hubbard wrote in his journal on May 7, 1941, "close to the earth, out-of-doors, simple and active, a way I can live in honor. How this can come about I do not see now. I shudder to think it may be only an idea." Harlan was forty-one years old, an artist whose work had gained no recognition, a sometime carpenter and construction worker, a solitary wanderer on the Ohio River and in the hills and woods of his native northern Kentucky. He found strength in solitude and joy in nature, but his loneliness and despair were intense. Then Anna Eikenhout entered his life. She was an accomplished musician, a scholar of French and German, a librarian. Together, Harlan wrote, they were a blend of "roughness and refinement." He was earthy, raw-boned, intense, and shy, a wildness about him. Anna, two years younger than Harlan, was an elegant, graceful woman, poised, feminine, and beautiful. They were each adventurous, imaginative, resourceful; they dreamed of living extraordinary lives. In the spring of 1943 Harlan and Anna were married, and soon they took their lives to the river. Harlan wrote, "We went to the riverbank, built a shantyboat, and began a new life together."

A man and a woman fulfilling their dreams, creating together a free-flowing, natural, independent life, making their home on the river, drifting with the current down to the sea—this is the story Harlan Hubbard told in *Shantyboat: A River Way of Life*. Then, extending their journey for a year into the wild, lush bayou country of Louisiana, Harlan and Anna basking in their adventurous success, discovering its meaning while exploring a strange new land—this is the story Harlan tells in *Shantyboat on the Bayous*. It is both a sequel to *Shantyboat* and a prelude to *Payne Hollow: Life on the Fringe of So-*

ciety, Harlan's testament to the homesteading life he and Anna went on to create in a remote, secluded notch in the Kentucky hills along the Ohio. The Hubbards settled at Payne Hollow in 1952 and lived there until their deaths, Anna's in 1986, and Harlan's in 1988. These books comprise an autobiographical whole, Harlan Hubbard's account of the life he shared with Anna, self-created and self-sustained, difficult and joyful, full of achievement and discovery, diligence, pleasure, and reward; "a life," Wendell Berry has written, "that is one of the finest accomplishments of our time."

Harlan had since childhood dreamed of living a river way of life. Growing up along the Ohio—Harlan was born January 4, 1900, in the rivertown of Bellevue, Kentucky—he was drawn to the shantyboaters he saw along its shores and later came to know, men who lived by the river's rhythms, beyond the reach of society's rules, "living on the fringes of life," Harlan wrote. "The simplicity and naturalness of their way of living fascinated me, and gave definite shape to the vague longing which the flowing river had inspired."

The river—and the writings of Thoreau—inspired in Harlan a "desire for a wilder life," open to all the elements of nature, the sun and sky and water and wind. When he was twenty-one years old Harlan experienced what he called a "revelation"—a stirring vision of the "truth" of his life: "At first there seemed to be two universes which I termed the world and the earth, in either of which I could choose to live. Then I saw there was but one, and that I was living on the earth looking directly into infinity."

This was the sense Harlan had of his life, and he carried it with him as he canoed on the river and hiked in the woods, making sketches of what he saw and felt, making his art of his native landscape. But he must live in the world too; Harlan felt so apart from "the world of men"—for they could not share his truth—that he imagined himself, like his art, unseen by the world, as if invisible, not-there in it. Only alone with his infinite vision did Harlan's life feel real to him: "Sometimes when slowly paddling or drifting, midway between the shores, I feel as detached from the world as a mote in space. The light of the sun, infinitely far away, strikes only me, it seems. . . . This is the way I go through the world of men; I observe and revel in forms and surfaces and color, entranced by them and all that formed them, but I slip through the mesh of the world without being caught, or even noticed."

Harlan lived this way for twenty years, until he joined his life to Anna's. Now he was no longer alone, and when he and Anna took their life to the river, he who had lived so apart from the world found his true place in it. Harlan wrote, "To achieve more perfect harmony with the river and at the same time live close to the earth and free from entanglement with this modern world, I became a shantyboater." For two years the Hubbards lived on their shantyboat tied to the river shore at Brent, Kentucky, a community of river people Harlan knew well. They became members of this community; with their shantyboat friends, Harlan and Anna fished and foraged and gardened for their food, gathered the river's driftwood to burn in their boat cabin's fires, and daily honored the sights and sounds and smells of their river way of life. Greeting "the morning of a new season," Harlan wrote in his journal, "The morning air was mild, with the song sparrow and Carolina wren tinkling away and the redbird whistling. The sun rose behind the bare trees across the river. I was out cutting wood early. . . . I breathed the morning air, listened to the birds and the *Catherine Davis* steaming past, blowing for the lock. I smelt the wood smoke from the fire I had kindled, and suddenly I felt that this was the realization of much that my life had been pointing to."

In December 1946, on a sudden rise in the river good for drifting, the Hubbards cast off from Brent, bound for New Orleans. Through four winters they drifted down the Ohio and the Missis-

sippi: "The tension and excitement," Harlan wrote, "the near ecstasy of drifting." In summertime, the river's current too slack for drifting, they tied their boat to the shore and made their home in new places on the land. All along the way the Hubbards explored new places and people, making a modern-day river odyssey: "Each time, it was a thrill to shove out into the current, to feel the life and power of the river.... We became a part of it, like the driftwood."

They reached their destination in May of 1950, having drifted 1,385 miles. But at New Orleans the Hubbards found that they could not yet give up their river way of life. Instead of ending their journey there as planned, they turned their shantyboat westward from the river, into still another new world, the bayous of Louisiana—"This strange new region," Harlan wrote, "where the land is almost water, and water is everywhere. We determined to leave the river and follow a new adventure in the land of the Cajun...."

In *Shantyboat: A River Way of Life* Harlan was an explorer, a seeker, his search intense and intimate: he was discovering *his* river, his own native stream. In *Shantyboat on the Bayous* Harlan is a relaxed, contented, appreciative traveler in a foreign land. He is excited by the bayous' extravagant array of hues and forms of nature, "the wispy greenness of the Spanish moss and the brilliant green of banana trees shooting into the blue sky." But he is no longer in thrall to the ecstatic tensions, the joyful rigors of his long drifting odyssey. That journey has been completed, and Harlan is pleased; now he is eager to share with us the simpler pleasures of leisurely traveling. In *Shantyboat on the Bayous* Harlan is a gracious, accommodating guide: "It was pleasant to sit on the main deck in the shade, and glide slowly through space and time with the smooth and gentle motion that only a boat in water can give. The sunny shores passed at a footpace. We could examine the varied grasses and plants which fringed the water—what a contrast between the elephant's-ear, with its broad, triangular leaves, and the soaring reeds—or look into the depths of the green, swampy forest hung with moss, or watch an approaching tug loom from a mere spot in the blue distance. If nothing attracted our attention we gazed with contentment down the long empty canal which narrowed until it was lost in the infinity of space."

Harlan and Anna are masterful travelers: sensitive, alert, perceptive, creative. Even if there is only space to observe, they are content and find infinity in it. They have so mastered the art of adventure that they are at home in the bayous, though they are wanderers in a strange new world: "One forgets the welcome the wilderness can give; it is like coming home. The vast emptiness around us was exciting. Two or three poles stuck in the muddy bottom by some fishermen were objects to which the eye and mind continually returned. In the level plane of earth and water, a few scrubby trees at the canal mouth were friendly and reassuring." Nothing is excluded from this vision of the welcoming wilderness: from "the vast emptiness" to "a few scrubby trees," the bayous extend a homecoming invitation, and Harlan and Anna accept it.

The Hubbards can feel so fully at home in the bayous—so excited by the place, yet so comfortable and secure in it—for reasons embodied in the qualities of character they bring to their experiencing of the world. Their admiration and respect, their reverence for all the forms of nature revealed to them enable Harlan and Anna to enact a meaningful and satisfying response. They open themselves fully to all the joys and wonders they find in this place on the earth they have come to, and they gratefully accept all the gifts it offers, accepting them for what they are, gifts of nature, freely given, freely to be received.

This was Harlan Hubbard's essential life-wisdom. Later in his life he would write in his journal: "Who is actually aware of the earth on which he lives? . . . How do they live without it? If I ever had to defend myself with a purpose, it would be to remind people of this earth on which they live, which they never see." Harlan makes us see it in *Shantyboat on the Bayous*: "Always the golden land was broken by water of the deepest blue where white birds waded." We see it and we feel it, the *presence* of the bayous, their vivid lushness haunting in its beauty, offering a promise timeless and eternal: "Like our voyage, the passage of time and the change of season seemed to have come to a stand. Who was it that, like us, had stayed his course to watch the ripening forest, where the cypress became an arrowhead of ruddy gold, where the maple, gum and oak blazed among the restrained colors of ash and hackberry; where the dark, glossy green of the live oak was a symbol of life everlasting?" This is Harlan's truth, his revelation made real, gracing this moment deep in the bayous.

There are two journeys being made in *Shantyboat on the Bayous*. Primarily, and delightfully, Harlan tells his tale of good traveling. As travel literature the book is excellent: entertaining and evocative, revealing of the new, and smoothly, beautifully written. On another level, underlying Harlan's narrative—surfacing here and there, never intrusive, but for the reader alert to it a constant, deepening presence—this book is a celebration of the Hubbards' journey of self-discovery. Drifting down the river Harlan and Anna had discovered the kind and quality of life they wished to live always; they discovered their future. Now, in repose on the bayous, they are savoring the success of their shantyboat adventure, exploring the depths of its meanings. "For the most part our days were quiet and unbroken," Harlan writes, "giving long-submerged thoughts and projects a chance to rise to the surface." They are exploring the reaches of their possibilities.

One project rising to the surface is *Shantyboat: A River Way of Life*. Harlan writes most of the book in the bayous. It is one of the culminations of his self-discovery: he becomes a writer, as well as a painter. And as he writes, among his rising thoughts are memories of his long time of loneliness, transformed by the presence of Anna

in his life, and of his urgent longings for meaning in his life, now fulfilled. Harlan's thoughts are of his happiness. There are no happier passages in all the writings of Harlan Hubbard than the ones in *Shantyboat on the Bayous* expressing his love for Anna and his contentment with himself. His love for Anna is expressed, shyly, subtly, and movingly, in Harlan's reverie-vision of the sunbonnet Anna wears as they glide through the bayous to shade her face from the hot southern sun. "Only her lovely chin and throat were visible under the pink-flowered sunbonnet," which Harlan recalls buying long before he knew Anna, during his solitary wanderings on the river. He saw it in the window of a rivertown shop, in a row of sunbonnets: "Attracted by their prettiness, as of old fashioned flowers, I had bought this one on a sudden impulse, thinking I might find someone to give it to." Now he has found that someone and celebrates her.

And Harlan celebrates himself, sharing with us a special birthday passage from his journal: "January 4, 1951—The warmest, sunniest birthday I can remember. . . . I am 51 years old today. As I was painting I was sure that what I could do, what I could see and how I could express it were worth even longer years of living. My writing is an unknown factor but it may amount to something. It is another expression of what I have felt and lived for. The creation of an environment in which it is possible to do this work, which allows the necessary time and freedom, peace of mind, happiness and security—this in itself is a success which is not always achieved."

"The creation of an environment": this will be the ultimate success achieved by Harlan and Anna Hubbard. At Payne Hollow they will create a life together fully, truly expressive of themselves, bountiful with self-fulfilling pleasures, art and music and good hard work, making their life from the river and the earth, making it whole: time and freedom, peace of mind, happiness and security. The Hubbards learned how to live this way drifting down the river; and on the bayous they enacted what they had learned. It was an opening into their future. In *Payne Hollow* Harlan recalled their last day in the bayous: as he and Anna "looked over the green shimmering landscape, it occurred to us that this was the sort of place we were seeking, remote and timeless, beyond the reach of highways, beyond today." The Hubbards found that place at Payne Hollow, and lived there for the rest of their lives—much as they lived in their year on the bayous. "It was a serene, contented time for us," Harlan wrote, "the unmarred days flowed smoothly into one another."

Don Wallis

Shantyboat ON THE Bayous

I

Our shantyboating began on the Ohio River with no more thought of cruising into the bayou country of southern Louisiana than of navigating the upper Amazon. In fact, we undertook this venture with no definite intentions of any kind, except a vague notion of drifting downstream as natural as a piece of driftwood and as heedless of an ultimate destination. We went down to the river in the hope of realizing a long-cherished desire to live close to it, with nothing between us and the stream we loved.

I was a natural for a shantyboat life, having that strange inclination to live apart from the established system, to provide what was necessary—and little more than that—by the labor of my own hands; to live in the hard way, much out-of-doors and in something of a wilderness. The riverbank was the only vestige of a frontier accessible to me. Also, I was attracted to it as an artist, a painter of sorts. Over a long period of years I had been painting the Ohio River in various phases, and a shantyboat seemed the most fitting studio.

With this background it is to be wondered at that I did not take to the river sooner, but I was kept from it by real or imaginary hindrances until I married. This event usually puts an end to such unconventional aspirations as shantyboating; nor had Anna ever shown any tendencies in that direction. Had not the city in which she was librarian been situated on the Ohio River, and had I not been an occasional visitor to the library, she would no doubt have been content to spend the rest of her life on land, with no suspicion of the rich experience we were to share. Yet it was she who suggested, soon after we were married, that we build a shantyboat and live on the river. Perhaps she thought it best to get this notion out of my system at once. At any rate, she made an excellent shantyboat wife, and the river life, so limited in some respects and yet so free, brought out unsuspected capabilities and developed innate strains of character.

Neither of us knew what we were getting into when we went down to the riverbank that autumn and built our little shantyboat. It was an exciting and joyous experience from the beginning, but we soon learned that a river life demanded more than we had anticipated. You can't move onto a boat from a house on land, even from one so informal as an artist's studio, and feel at home right away. If shantyboaters are not born—as was the case with us—they must be made, and the process takes time. For two rich years our boat lay moored to the bank at the spot where she was built, while we became adapted to an amphibious existence and learned something of the ups and downs of shantyboating. Then, as we drifted away to begin the downstream voyage and saw the familiar landing merge into the endless shore, a new dimension of river life was opened to us. To navigate a heavy boat controlled only by arm power on the swift waters of winter is an exacting sport, hazardous at times, full of excitement and unexpected happenings. Drifting became a passion with us in the four winters of our trip down the Ohio and Mississippi rivers. During the quiet intervals of summer we were content to lay over at some rural landing with at least one foot on shore, where we made a garden and became for the time members of the farm community around us.

When at length New Orleans was reached, our shantyboat life was in full swing. The river had worked its change, and to live with flowing water beneath us seemed the natural and most desirable way. Our first New Orleans harbor, far enough upstream to be in the country, was in a quiet lagoon behind an abandoned levee. It was a relief to be out of the current for a time; yet the flooded Mississippi was still close to us, for we were moored just inside the narrow reef which had once been the top of a levee. Outside it, a few yards from our deck, the winter rains and melted snows of half the United States were silently rolling toward the sea.

These were sweet days. In the southern spring the air was soft and balmy, the sun warm. Mockingbirds and thrashers sang in the greening brush of our narrow island. Along the mainland rode the new levee where cows grazed on the greenest of grass. We sometimes rowed across the narrow lagoon in our johnboat, and each time, on climbing the slope, we were astonished to see a road, houses and fields all lying at a lower level than the water. Sometimes our errand was to the nearby country store and post office, or we roamed the countryside gathering greens and picking dewberries along the railroad embankment, much as we would have done in Kentucky, although there was so much here that was strange to us. A few times, leaving the dogs on the boat, we boarded a bus and rode to New Orleans to make our acquaintance with that unique city, delighted with the novel and exotic character of all that we saw.

Most of the time, however, we were content to remain on our small island. The shantyboat itself is like an island, a floating one, self-contained and ever the same through all the shifting scenes and circumstances of the voyage. We had not drifted far from our home port before we discovered how delightful and satisfying it is to travel and not be obliged to leave anything behind. All our wanted possessions were with us—tools, books, dogs, bicycle, scraps of material, summer and winter clothing, violin, viola, 'cello, and equipment for painting. In the beginning our favorite pursuits were somewhat neglected because we were occupied almost wholly with the novelty of living on water, with completing our boat and learning river ways. Now, after more than five years of river life, the days seemed unaccountably longer and nothing we wanted to do need be crowded out. This was due in part to the efficiency of our boat, which had become almost part of ourselves. The home-made gadgets had been worked out to a fine point and tested by use, everything on board had found its proper place, and order was maintained with little effort.

Even with this broad margin of leisure the hours were precious as ever and we were always doing something, even if it were nothing more than to sit in the sun and watch the river. It was warm enough now to eat our midday meal on deck, and we often lingered there to indulge in that time-consuming pleasure of reading aloud; though these hours were redeemed to some extent by the industrious listener, whose hands were busy at "knitting" a fish net or other shantyboat handicraft, or at catching up on some household chore which otherwise might be tedious, like mending or cracking and picking out nuts. We had frequent sessions with the 'cello and violin, playing duets or pieces we arranged for two strings. Often we played quartets, two parts at a time—an excellent way to study these works. I whittled wood blocks which we printed together, and I often set up my easel, a driftwood plank wedged between floor and ceiling.

During these happy days we were disturbed only by the thought that they could not long continue. Spring would all too soon give way to the heat of summer, the river would fall—it had already started down—the water would drain off the batture, as the strip just outside the levee is called, and we would be forced out into the open river, with no protection from wind and waves, with a muddy wilderness for a shore. Also, we knew that in time we would want to be on the move and see new shores. The difficulty was, which way to go? The Mississippi below New Orleans is no place for a shantyboat because its unbroken shores afford no protection from the waves of the many ocean ships which enter and leave the port. We thought of having our boat towed back up the river, but that would be a tame ending to a voyage which began with the exciting drift down with the river's current. Of course, we might sell out and return overland to our starting place, after the tradition of flatboat days which made New Orleans the final port; but to give up shantyboating at this high point was unthinkable, and we had no intention of abandoning our boat just when it had reached its full development.

The course we finally decided to attempt became quite reasonable after due consideration, and it was such a logical solution of our problem that we wondered why there should ever have been any hesitation; yet to leave the river and go westward into the bayou country had at first seemed a wild and desperate move. It would mean a long voyage on the Intracoastal Waterway, which was a canal dug through an uninhabitable swamp, from all that we had ever heard of it, and not inviting or friendly to shantyboaters. The idea appealed to us only because it would allow the even rhythm of our shantyboating to continue. Our outlook changed completely, however, after one glimpse of the bayou country, the day I went to Barataria. Then we became enthusiastic about the voyage, and eager to reach those waters which promised so much.

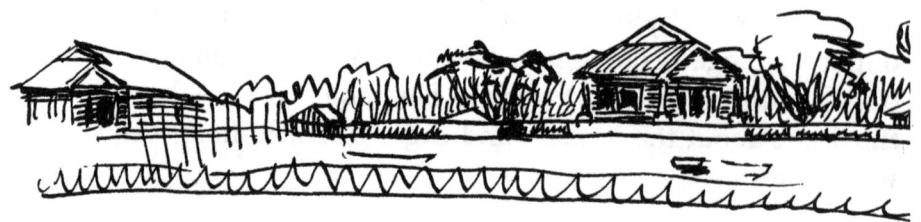

II

It was from a road map that we got the idea of making a sortie to Barataria, which was marked as a small town on Bayou Barataria and only twenty miles from New Orleans. Thus by a single day's trip we could have a look at one of the Bayous and also at the Intracoastal Waterway, which follows Bayou Barataria for a ways. We hoped that even this brief contact would make the bayou country real instead of imaginary and inform us whether or not the Intracoastal was feasible for shantyboat navigation.

We decided that I should make this trip alone, a circumstance rare enough to make any day memorable. Of course, I had frequently left Anna on the boat while I went exploring new shores at which we had landed, times when she preferred staying on board to clambering over the rough banks or through the woods in wind and rain. Happily for both of us, she never minded being alone. In fact, she liked it once in a while, for the chance it afforded to do little things for herself, to spread her work about the cabin or practice on the 'cello without having to stop, clear the deck, and cook a meal; though I never could see any reason why she shouldn't do these things even when I was around. Such trivial circumstances make a difference, however. For instance, the dogs always went with me on scouting expeditions ashore, while on this trip to Barataria I would be entirely by myself. Skipper and Sambo had expected to go along and were all excited about it, but their hopefulness vanished when they saw me taking the bicycle from under the tarpaulin on the roof, where it was stored with the washtubs and a lot of stuff that wouldn't fit inside the cabin.

I was sorry to disappoint the dogs, but once away from the boat I realized how good it was to be all alone, at least for a while. As I pedaled along the road behind the levee I was prepared for great adventures. Nothing exciting happened, however. I only went to Barataria and back again; but the sight of that strange low region where land and water are so close was enough for even so special a day as this.

I could have bicycled the whole way to Barataria and return, nearly eighty miles, but thinking to travel faster I took a city bus when I reached the outer end of its route, leaving the wheel in a gas station. The bus carried me down the west shore of the Mississippi, the side opposite to New Orleans. With the road map for a guide, I left the bus and started walking out the Barataria road, wishing I had the bicycle again; but an obliging driver picked me up and carried me all the way.

The road abruptly left the metropolitan district along the river and traversed low fields and woods. It was not long before houses were sighted ahead, not city buildings but small cottages set in the line of trees that marked the bayou. This was Barataria, whose very name suggests the meandering of currentless water through a flat country.

At first sight I knew that I had come upon a place unlike any I had ever seen. Though but a few miles away, there was nothing about it to remind me of the Mississippi.

The road followed the stream, a road on each side much of the way, connected at rather long intervals by low bridges. At the very first crossing, the road was blocked while the bridge swung open to let a fishing boat pass, a white trawler with a rakish mast. Though tempted to get out of the car right there, I stayed with my ride until the end of the road. Beyond lay a marshy prairie, too unstable for road or houses. The bayou kept on southward and I longed to follow it as it wound through the tall grass, to see it widen into desolate bays and not so far distant enter the open water of the Gulf of Mexico. But this day, being landbound, I strolled back along the road, following short lanes to the bayou, leaning over bridge rails to watch the water, the fishermen, sea birds and boats.

The little houses were strung along close to the water on both sides of the bayou, not compact enough to form a recognizable town, yet never so far apart that it might be called open country. I could not make out which way the houses faced. In most cases the apparent front was toward the road, but every house had a well-used path to the shore, ending in a dock or boathouse.

Though not far from New Orleans, Barataria might have been a remote settlement, it was so self-contained and showed so little influence of the city. The people were busy about their own affairs, and seemed to have no interest in outsiders. The common use of French astonished me. It was spoken by the men at work building a new trawler; women chatted in French over the fence, and children along the road shouted in a strange lingo. Barataria was in the land of the Cajun. One could tell that by the names on mail boxes, on boats, on the stores.

I was happy to see a place so thoroughly boat-minded. The store in which I bought some crackers and cheese for lunch was a combination country store and boat store. It faced the bayou and had a dock for waterborne customers. Everyone seemed to have a boat and to use it for going places. No one rowed, however; they paddled about in pirogues. I had never before had a good look at a pirogue. It is a little slip of a boat with barely enough freeboard to keep the water from coming over the side. The occupant sits midway on the bottom with no width to spare. Using a single short paddle, with knees sticking up to keep a sack of groceries or perhaps a youngster from falling overboard, he, or she, nonchalantly skims along the smooth water.

Another type of boat of which I saw many on Barataria was a skiff with an inboard engine. They were used by fishermen, and some were quite small, perhaps only twelve feet in length, with a tiny engine that popped along and steamed like a teakettle, having, it seems, no circulating cooling system. Some of the newer boats were "air-cools," others were virtually speed boats with powerful marine engines. The bayou was a lively place with the many small boats coming and going, an occasional trawler or oyster lugger running up the bayou loaded, or stopped at a dock for supplies before continuing on its way to the outer waters.

Since the Intracoastal follows Bayou Barataria for several miles, I had a chance to see what sort of traffic used this route. The tows passed more frequently than they did on the rivers, but the tugs were smaller than river towboats. Yet I saw one big New Orleans tug with five barges. These were strung out in a line and the last one dragged the bank—a hazard on this part of the bayou which makes it impossible to maintain a dock. All boats must

be pulled out or moored in slips cut into the bank. A cruising shantyboat would have to navigate the Intracoastal with caution. I did see some boats on which people lived, but they were moored in protected water. Nevertheless I saw no reason why we should not bring our shantyboat over this route, and the frequency of safe harbors in side canals and behind islands was reassuring.

With so much to be seen, the few hours I had to spend on Barataria passed quickly. In midafternoon I turned homeward, making the first stage of the trip in a bakery truck which was bound for the "front." The driver was talkative and I learned some of the fine points of bread delivery. He was taking home a basket of crabs bought from a Cajun fisherman. "I don't see how he can sell them so cheap," he remarked.

Eager as I was to get back to the shantyboat, I interrupted the homeward ride on the bicycle to pick a cabbage head or two from one of the truck farms along the road. The sun had set when I came abreast of our landing and pushed the bicycle up the grassy slope of the levee. As always after an absence, however brief, the sight of the river was breath-taking. It was immense as infinity in the blue-gray mist which dimmed the far shore. Across the narrow lagoon the shantyboat would have been lost in the twilight except for candlelight flickering in the window. I called, "Yo-ho-oo." The dogs began to yelp and oars thumped in the johnboat. Soon Anna was with me.

"How was it?" she asked.

"Wonderful," I said, "It's the place for us."

A gentle rain fell that evening and the open fire gave warmth and cheer to our cabin. Instead of our usual reading aloud, I told of Bayou Barataria, of the fishermen, of pirogues and skiffs on the busy waterway, of the shores deep in the shade of live oaks, of the old cottages whose sides and roofs were weathered to a silvery gray which sparkled in the sun. As I recalled the place, its contrasts seemed more vivid—the light and shade on the road of white shells, the wispy grayness of Spanish moss, and the brilliant green of banana trees shooting into the blue sky, the white fishing boats with masts and trim of bright red, blue or orange, the new boxlike dwellings next to the heavy-shuttered homes of the old days.

Before going to bed we read a little in a tattered fragment of a book—once a volume of Andersen's fairy tales—which I had found by the roadside that day. In this mood we recalled tales and legends of the bayous, heard along the river or read in forgotten books, and in our sleepy minds they became enchanted streams leading into a country beyond reality.

III

A shantyboater learns to accept the weather as it comes and wait it out. Otherwise we might have been impatient during the period of wind and rain which now kept us in our harbor and postponed our departure. Though eager to reach our new cruising ground, we settled down contentedly enough to indoor occupations, enjoying the extra hours of reading and music, writing and painting. The voyage ahead was never out of our minds, however, and we prepared ourselves for it by studying a book of detailed maps of the Intracoastal Waterway obtained from the New Orleans office of the U. S. Engineers on our last visit to the city. The very names of places in the Acadian land were alluring—Bayou Terrebonne, Cypremort, Vermilion Bay—and with much pleasure we cruised in imagination along the Intracoastal. Here we ran close to the shore of the Gulf, in another place we would cross a lake or follow a winding bayou, and it was possible to leave the main route and thread our way along Bayou Lafourche, Bayou Teche, and other fabulous streams of whose location and course we had hitherto no idea whatever.

The course of the Intracoastal westward from New Orleans is roughly parallel to the Gulf of Mexico. The gateway from the Mississippi River is the Harvey Lock, a lock being necessary at this point because of the difference of level between the canal, which is sea level, and the river, which still has nearly a hundred miles to flow before it reaches the Gulf. From the lock, the Harvey Canal runs to Bayou Barataria, the first of the bayous which form links in the Intracoastal chain.

Since our shantyboat was moored some twenty miles up the river from the Harvey Lock, this short drift on the Mississippi would be the first leg of our voyage. It was a tricky run, however, first under the high bridge from which we had, on our bus trips to the city, looked down on the swirling waters with misgiving; for we always lost some of our confidence during a long stay in a protected harbor. Below the bridge we would encounter the shipping of the port of New Orleans and have to make a definite landing, which is not easy when drifting in a swift current. Yet, when we prepared to leave and freed the boat from shore, all thought of hazards vanished like the morning mist. We shoved away from land, felt the current take hold of our boat with a gentle, effortless force and carry it onward. The old surge of joy at being adrift rose in us again. Our minds were troubled only by the thought that we were soon to leave the river, the faithful companion which had thus far on our journey been constantly with us. For the last time we had given our boat to the river's current. Could the still waters of the bayou offer moments such as these?

Early in the afternoon we approached the lock, its exact location indicated to us by the tug *Atlas*, which turned in just ahead of us. With our oars we broke the shantyboat loose from the grip of the current and pulled toward the lock gate which was being held open for us.

From within the lock we looked back across the golden current of the river to the distant New Orleans shore, its docks and buildings. Then the lock gate closed and the last view of the Mississippi we were to have from the deck of our shantyboat was cut off. The water within the lock ebbed and the boat began its slow descent to sea level. Even the pinnacles of the New Orleans skyline sank behind the black gate which seemed to be rising into the sky. No trace of the river remained. Though so recently left, the Mississippi was already far behind us, and our long drifting on its current was of the past.

The lockman on top of the wall parleyed with Anna and me

as we stood on the deck, gradually shifting our handholds to lower rungs of the ladder embedded in the concrete.

The man was filling out a printed form.

"Where from?" he asked.

"Brent, Kentucky." We had to locate Brent by telling him it was on the Ohio River near Cincinnati.

His next questions were off the record.

"Did you come all that way in that boat?" We did feel a long way from home.

"Did you come down the Mississippi without a motor?" We assured him that we had drifted with the river's current all the way, nearly fourteen hundred miles.

Next the lockman asked, "Where are you bound?"

This was a hard one to answer, for I did not know just where we were going. "To the bayou country" would not be specific enough for the record. With a sudden inspiration I came up with "Morgan City." This was the name of a town which had been mentioned to us by river people whose wanderings had taken them west of the Mississippi.

We were spared the necessity of classifying our craft, for the lockman listed it as a quarterboat—a rather stilted term, we thought, for such an outfit as ours, makeshift at best, now battered and scarred by the four-year voyage.

The questions relating to cargo were skipped over. Then, after putting down the dimensions of our craft, twenty-four feet long by ten wide, and guessing the tonnage, the man on the lock solemnly announced, "The toll will be $25."

For a moment I almost believed him. After this bewildering day of drifting down through the New Orleans harbor, dodging tugs and ferryboats, and at last leaving the river to enter the narrow canal which would lead us into a land where all was new and strange, we were prepared to believe almost anything; and there was a toll canal somewhere around New Orleans, though I thought it was on the other side. Before I could say anything to make a fool of myself it became apparent that the man was joking, and we laughed with him.

Later we wondered why the Harvey Lock had been so particular about this formal questioning. I even had to sign the manifest. The Ohio River locks had put us through with only some offhand conversation. The making of a record pleased us, however, and we looked on it as an official recognition of our shantyboat voyage. It came at an appropriate time, too—at the beginning of this venture into waters which did not flow.

After a slow drop of some fourteen feet, our downward motion ceased. Then the gate ahead was opened, the lockman waved us out. We quickly took our accustomed places for rowing: I in the johnboat ahead, so that I could tow and guide the unwieldy shantyboat, and Anna pulling at the sweeps on the main deck. This was the arrangement used on the rivers, and by our combined efforts we had been able to control the boat when drifting and row it slowly through slack water, unless wind interfered.

The tug *Atlas*, which had entered the lock ahead of us, dashed away down the canal blowing three short blasts for the bridges beyond the lock—the first carrying a railroad across the canal, the second a highway. The *Atlas* was soon through both and out of sight. The bridge tenders, seeing our boat pulling out of the lock, held the spans open for us. There would have been plenty of time to lower the bridges before we came near, and we wished they would do this so that we could rest and take it easy; but thinking of the traffic piling up on the blocked highway, we rowed hard and steadily. Straining our arms, and barely moving at that, we passed a signboard listing the places westward on the canal. There was Morgan City, 95 miles; a far way, it seemed at that moment.

At length we made it under the second bridge, the span was closed, and the pent-up cars, trucks and streetcars stampeded across. We could relax now and look about us. The canal widened to form a long basin on which were many boats—small tugs and fishing boats mostly—moving along the canal or lying at the docks belonging to waterside industries. The whole scene was full of activity. Since we were accustomed to wide rivers, all this seemed to be on a small scale, and much more intimate than the towering piers and ocean ships of the vast Mississippi. We felt at home among the small boats, though no shantyboats were to be seen. Indeed, our outlandish rig being rowed along the Harvey Canal must have been an unusual sight. Unconcerned with the impression we might be making on the rest of the world, we crept slowly along, delighted with all we saw.

First on the right were some trawlers and oyster boats clustered about the dock of a sea-food packing house, which gave an authentic fishy smell to the air. Near the bridge was a U.S. Engineer depot, indicating that, however wild and strange the waterways toward the west might be, they would be marked by the familiar red and black buoys. At one dock along the canal a bargeload of white shells was being unloaded onto a great heap, just as sand and gravel are handled on the Ohio River. Farther along we passed the terminal of a towing company, a waiting tug at its landing. At one dock was a gas station for boats, at another a diesel engine sales and service. Everything seemed to pertain to boats, though we did see a lumber yard, a shop where galvanizing was done, and a cooperage company whose barrels were oil drums. The oil industry figured largely in the Harvey basin. There were storage yards and landings for oil companies, and in one area oil derricks were being assembled. Some of the signs, such as "The Harvey Mud Company," "Driller's Mud," and "The Oil Well Cementing Company," puzzled us greenhorns.

All the while we kept looking for the boatyard and slip mentioned by the lock tender as a possible mooring for our shantyboat. This clanging marine ways, where some large tugs and a river towboat were pulled out for repairs, could not be the place. More promising was the smaller shipyard farther along, whose ways, parallel to the canal, sloped to a square basin or slip, the bayou term for any harbor, great or small, which is cut into the bank. The slip was nearly filled with fishing boats, but we worked in among them and tried to land at an open place on the far side. This was apparently on the property of the sulphur company which was next to the shipyard, for a man immediately came out of the office and told us to keep off in no uncertain terms.

Although the part of the slip near the marine ways was crowded, we moved over there and anchored our shantyboat among the trawlers and powerboats, where it was as conspicuously out of place as a horse and buggy in a parking lot. We expected to be ordered away, but no one paid any attention to us. In fact, scarcely a person was to be seen, and no work was going on. We were quite sure the day was not Sunday. I went over to talk with a man who had been observing us from the deck of a large cabin boat, built for speed and rough water, which bore the name *Yippee,* of Chicago. He said that no one was working because the day was Good Friday, a holiday among the French fishermen which would last until Monday. We did not trust too much this man's assurance that no one would mind our staying in the slip, even though the *Yippee* had a gangplank ashore and appeared to have been there for some time; but the weekend at least would be peaceful and undisturbed, so we made ourselves at home.

It was our hope that we could lay over in this convenient harbor long enough to refit and make ready for the voyage ahead. Some basic changes had to be made in our manner of navigation. River techniques must be given up because of the impossibility of drifting in the still water or slow, changeable current of the canal and bayous. That we could never get anywhere by our own efforts was made plain by the tedious haul from the lock that very afternoon. The only solution appeared to be a motorboat of some kind, and it did not appeal to us. Drifting had been a happy and satisfying experience largely because it was as natural as the river itself. Moreover, we distrusted motors in general, believing that they are often not worth their trouble and expense.

When work was resumed at the boatyard on Monday we tried to keep out of the way and were gratified to find that no one seemed to take any notice of us. Our uneasiness vanished, also the feeling of urgency. We relaxed into a shantyboat tempo, confident that the problem of an engine for towing power could be worked out satisfactorily, given a little time.

Though eager to get on with our voyage, we welcomed the chance to tarry a while at Harvey, which to us, so thoroughly river-minded, had the novelty of a foreign port. Our first interest was the fishing boats. They seemed to be mainly of two types: one for the open sea and rough water—a sharp-bowed, high-sided craft with cabin well forward, mast and boom aft; the other, which never left the bays except in fair weather, had an almost flat bottom for less draft, a lower freeboard, rounded bow and bilge. The mast was forward, the small cabin at the stern. This boat appealed to us greatly; of perhaps an older and more traditional design, it had the innate, natural grace of a boat perfectly adapted to its service. Both kinds were shrimp trawlers. The short mast and boom were used for handling the trawl net, which was often hung up to dry, resembling a black sail loosely furled.

The oyster boats, since they worked in shallow water, were similar to the bay trawlers but without masts. When they came in, their decks, nearly awash, would be piled with crusty-looking oysters in a long heap from bow to cabin, kept from sliding overboard by a bulwark of sacked oysters around the edge.

Some of the boats in the slip seemed to be biding their time, as we were. One such lay near us, a broad-beamed, flat-bottomed open hull belonging to a fisherman, one of the numerous Landrys, who came down to pump out the rainwater after each shower. His homemade bilge pump was so simple that I could not understand how it worked so well. He referred to his boat as a skiff, a term which among the fishermen seems to include any undecked boat with a model bow, regardless of size.

From our berth in the slip we had no view up or down the canal. The passing boats appeared in the opening before us and were gone. One could never guess what would come next, but there were no long gaps in the procession. A big, seagoing tug might be followed by a workboat on its way to some narrow bayou. Only one steam tug passed, an old-timer which corresponded to the river steamboats. The tugs were more numerous than the fishing boats. They towed their barges in a line astern, a novel sight to us, accustomed to river towing, which is not really towing because the river towboat shoves the barge or fleet of barges ahead of it.

We saw quite a few river towboats on the canal, some of them old friends from the Upper Ohio—the *Reliance*, perhaps, with barges of steel pipe for Texas. When these boats returned from the west with barges loaded with oil, sugar, rice, sulphur, scrap iron, or unrecognizable cargo, they were at the foot of the hill with perhaps two thousand miles of upstream work ahead of them on the Mississippi and Ohio Rivers.

A large proportion of canal traffic had to do with the oil industry. Not only the products of oil field and refinery, but machinery, supplies and personnel were moved by water. We often saw a complete oil derrick go by mounted on a barge, or another barge might contain a battery of steam boilers which would supply power for some offshore or marshland drilling. The oil companies employed many types of workboats and crew boats, from large, fast cruisers—yachts, some of them—to a ridiculous craft which was a sort of amphibious tractor, its four large wheels being watertight drums with cleats on them to propel the vehicle when afloat. It looked like a magnified wooden toy, but its capabilities were demonstrated when later we saw this odd machine in action. It was being used by surveyors to run lines in the marsh, and it went through everything in its path—water, mud and tall grass.

The never-ending traffic on the canal, the din and bustle of the workshops along the shores, gave an atmosphere of tense activity to the Harvey basin which was not favorable to quiet shantyboat living. In fact, mere living seemed aimless, hardly worth while, and we felt a little guilty enjoying ourselves in the sun, watching as bystanders the flow of traffic, the busy men and the progress of work on the boats. At times the discord about us became almost too much—the hammering, riveting, sawing, the ceaseless throb of diesel engines, the noise of trucks on the unpaved road along the canal, from which dust sifted into our cabin—and we longed for a quiet haven in the open country where the air would be clean and the nights dark and silent; where the river's peace would return to us, almost as a living companion.

It is a shantyboater's consolation, when a situation is not to his liking, that he will soon be moving on to more favored shores—a practical application in a small way of a principle that has cheered unhappy people for a long time. He has an additional blessing in the continuity of his life. Through all his shifting about, now among other boats and people, now in a desolate reach of river or behind an island with not even a navigation light for company at night, now amid the din of the city, as we were at this time, he carries with him intact his home and familiar trappings, his established pattern of living, not affected by the hazards of travel or by any current unpleasantness.

Thus we were cheered by the thought that the confusion about us was a passing phase and that we would soon reach the peaceful wilderness which lay not far ahead. Yet we did not let the contemplation of future happiness get in the way of our enjoyment of the present moment and place. After all, the irritations at Harvey were really a small and transient part of the days we spent there. The mornings, for instance, were as fresh and inspiring as if the sun had risen over country hills. Its first rays were warm, the air was soft as it is only along the Gulf, the sky was of the southern sea. Before industry began to stir, the placid water reflected boats and buildings which seemed still asleep. In the evening came another tranquil period. When the day's work was over I would row across the quiet slip to the machine shop where there was a tap from which I could get drinking water. I picked up a few assorted galvanized nails dropped under the hulls of boats on the ways, the dogs searched out scraps where the workmen had eaten their lunches. The watchman was a friend of ours.

On our way down the rivers we had avoided the cities, preferring to land above or below them along country shores, from which the city could be reached only by an arduous trip beginning with a climb through the brush and a long walk over a dusty or muddy road. From our present landing in the Harvey Canal, however, New Orleans was within easy reach, by our standards, and we made the most of it. The Mississippi River was crossed on the old steam stern-wheel ferry *A. Baldwin*, which seemed never to be in a hurry. Its engines were of the simplest kind, and we watched the moving pitmans and felt the pounding of the paddle wheel with a nostalgic pleasure. As we looked down on the beloved muddy water of the river, we felt its old attraction, and might have been disturbed had we not before us the prospect of another voyage.

New Orleans itself has a strong steamboat flavor, or perhaps we saw only that side of it. Our personalized sightseeing took us mostly along the widespread waterfront, where we sauntered about the unguarded, unrestricted docks, never tiring of watching ships loading and unloading, enchanted by strange cargoes and names of far-off ports.

Anna took advantage of our access to the city by arranging for 'cello lessons. Her teacher, recommended by the music librarian of Sophie Newcomb College, was a member of the New Orleans symphony orchestra, and since her charming old house was but a short streetcar ride from the ferry landing, Anna could take a lesson every other day. It was a strange sight to see her carrying the 'cello in its black case out through the littered shipyard and down a road wholly given over to industry and construction.

Far from its being submerged by this city environment, our shantyboat life went on in its normal way, much as if we had been tied up at some rural landing. No doubt we would have found a spot to make a garden if our stay were going to be long enough for a harvest. As it was, we foraged about for wild crops—dewberries along the canal banks, ripening in the April sun, and fresh shoots of pokeweed by the roadside. Though we did no fishing in the canal at Harvey, we caught shrimp in a small net such as we had used on the Mississippi, made of a grass sack stretched flat and held at the corners by two arched willow withes. There was good picking in the driftwood which floated about the canal or littered the shore line.

Few places are so completely urban that some remnant of wilderness or waste land cannot be found nearby. Along the Harvey Canal the cleared strip did not extend far inland. Every morning I slipped under the fence that enclosed the shipyard and after a short walk entered a swampy forest. The dogs caught a raccoon a few rods from the boat.

Although in no hurry to get on with our voyage, we kept mulling over the possible ways of towing our shantyboat. An engine in the boat itself had been ruled out at once as an unthinkable intrusion. The simplest solution of the problem would be an outboard motor fastened to our johnboat. We decided against an outboard, however, fearing that its small, high-speed propeller would not develop efficiently the required towing power.

We have no fondness for a motor of any kind, unless it could be a steam engine, but a small motorboat having an inboard engine would be least objectionable. Though not caring how slowly it towed us along, we must have a boat that we could live with on pleasant terms, one with a sturdy engine that could be run all day without strain on either itself or us.

We had noticed a few skiffs belonging to fishermen which might answer our requirements, but when we began to look in earnest nothing suitable could be found. Remembering the number of small boats I had seen on Bayou Barataria, I determined to extend the search there. When I mentioned this to Landry, the fisherman, he offered me a ride to Barataria in his skiff—the heavy, broad-beamed hull moored near our boat—which was to be towed down the canal. I would have been eager to go with him, even without a reason for the trip. Next morning the trawler *Margery C*, her repairs at the shipyard having been completed, took the skiff in tow and, after much heaving and shouting, got under way. As we rounded into the canal I waved to Anna, who waved back from the deck of the shantyboat; and the little shantyboat, with its faded red hull and once-white cabin, seemed to be wishing me "Bon Voyage" in its own way. All was bound up in a feeling of love and comradeship.

It was an interesting trip on the *Margery C*, with its Cajun crew and passengers—I could not tell which was which; nor could I understand their animated, unceasing conversation in Cajun French. They showed little curiosity about me, a stranger, or about my bicycle, which I was taking for the return trip, although it must have been a novelty on a trawler. Only one stop was made before Barataria was reached, at a point in the woods where all of us went ashore to cut and carry on board a quantity of long, straight willow poles—to be used by the fishermen to mark their oyster beds in the shallow bays and lakes, I was told.

They put me ashore at Cherami's boatyard, the *Margery C* continuing her way toward the Gulf. I now began my search, riding along the roads which follow the bayou and crossing on a bridge from one side to the other, stopping at every likely place to ask if they knew of a small skiff for sale. It seemed that the only boats available were too large, too powerful, or too expensive. At length a young fellow from Bayou des Oies, or Goose Bayou, took me to see a boat belonging to a friend of his. This friend worked for one of the oil companies which operated in the Barataria region, though he was from a family of fishermen. He lived in a neat white cottage, and a few steps from his back door, at a flimsy pier, was a small, gray-painted skiff which took my eye at once. It had an honest look about it, a character which promised willing and faithful service. Though heavily built and broad of beam, it was a good-looking boat, I thought, with graceful lines.

The engine, small and unobtrusive, made a pleasant chucking noise on a trial run. The boat was slow, of deep draft, and awkward to handle, but these defects would not keep it from being an efficient towboat.

I kept thinking of the skiff as I rode homeward, but this did not interfere with my making the usual collection of stuff along the way. Thus I arrived at the boat with some roadside dewberries, fresh oysters from a little sea-food shop, an empty case for sun glasses, lost from a car, a few deep-orange lilies, a sack of ripe bananas (a bargain from one of the roadside hucksters whose wagons are to be seen on streets and roads about New Orleans), a bunch of parsley picked from a field, and for the dogs a rabbit freshly killed by traffic.

Anna was eager to hear of my day's adventures. After I had told her about the skiff it became the subject for much consideration and discussion which ended in our decision to buy it, as we both knew we would from the beginning. Accordingly, a few days after the first trip, I bicycled down to Barataria with the money in my pocket. The owner of the skiff now seemed hesitant about selling it; not from any unwillingness to part with it, I made out, but from some scruples as to its suitability for towing our shantyboat. He did not know how slowly we would be content to travel. At last the deal was made, I put the bicycle in the skiff and managed to get the engine started. It did not miss a beat, nor did I touch it, all the way back to Harvey.

The skiff now became our prime concern. We must become acquainted with it, understand the operation of the engine, learn to handle it, and above all put boat and motor in first-class shape. In all this I was advised and assisted by the skipper of the *Yippee*. He and his wife were friendly people and good neighbors. From Chicago they had cruised down the Illinois and Mississippi Rivers in their large cabin boat, which had been a naval patrol vessel of some sort. It had sunk in the river across from New Orleans, and when it was raised they brought it into this shipyard for repairs. From what I could see, the *Yippee* would never run again; the twin engines, not overhauled after their ducking in river water, were badly rusted. It was an inconvenient boat for living, with the cabin below decks and not much space considering the size of the boat. Yet our jaunty friend walked the deck with pride and show of authority. He always had plenty of time, which was good for us and for the many others whom he readily assisted with his advice, tools and even labor. Since I knew little about motorboats, I ran aboard the *Yippee* many times during the day with some part that needed repair or explanation; or my errand would be to borrow a tool, or just to talk about boats and engines.

Our skiff was thirteen years old, built of cypress by Adam Dufresne on Bayou Barataria. The hull was staunch and sound, needing only a good scraping to remove the thick, hairlike marine growth below the water line. To accomplish this I raised one end out of the water at a time, using a chain hoist borrowed from the *Yippee*. When the stern was out I tightened the rudder.

The engine was thirteen years old, too. Gasoline engines do not last as long as cypress hulls, and this one showed its age. When we got to working on it so many defects showed up that I marveled at my good fortune in running it home from Barataria without a breakdown. It should have had a complete overhaul right then—cylinder rebored, new piston, rings and other parts. Instead, I did only enough to keep the engine running. Later as parts failed I fixed or replaced them one at a time, and consequently it was months before the engine ran well or dependably.

This was a simple affair for a gasoline engine—one cylinder, four-cycle, all working parts easily accessible. It had no clutch, no reverse, no crank, even. To start it you took hold of the exposed flywheel as best you could and turned it in a counterclockwise direction, which seemed backward to me, having cranked some automobiles in my day. When compression was reached, you flipped the heavy flywheel over and the engine popped off, if you were lucky.

I learned to understand the operation of this engine very well except for the ignition system, and of this I could at least locate and work on the component parts—a set of four dry batteries, a coil, timer and spark plug. Having been designed in the days of the Model T Ford, the engine used as many of its parts as possible—piston, rings, connecting rod, valves, coil. This made replacement easy, until the Model T passed out of existence.

I admired the simple devices used by the Cajun mechanic who had installed the engine in the boat. A rag tied around the propeller shaft looked like a makeshift way of keeping water from leaking in, yet I found it efficient and lasting if the rag were greased and then wrapped in the proper direction with relation to the turning of the shaft.

I soon developed an affection for the skiff and even for the engine, although my respect and trust in the engine were not unreserved. In its very nature it seemed to be working against itself, and its operation depended on so many close adjustments that I wondered that it ran at all. Yet even more to be marveled at is the intricate economic structure on which the engine must depend for fuel and service. What keeps that running without miss or backfire?

One day when I was not at home the superintendent of the boatyard appeared on the bank and asked Anna if we were waiting for repairs. This we took as a tactful and considerate way of informing us that we would not be welcome there indefinitely. Not ready to leave, I stalled for time; even asked for an estimate on having our shantyboat pulled out on the ways and its hull painted with copper paint—a protection against marine worms that would be necessary if we went into salt water. When told that I would not be allowed to do any of the work myself, I knew the cost would be above our shantyboat scale. The superintendent must have understood this, too, since he remarked that copper paint would not be needed if we stayed on the Intracoastal Waterway. After all, he did not mind our being in the slip for a short and limited time; but one shantyboat attracts another, and this was no place for such a colony.

I had also to make an explanation to the sulphur company, which was exerting pressure from the other side. It was time we were getting out of there. What puzzled us was the *Yippee*. It took up more space than our boat and no one seemed to mind its being there—perhaps because it did not look like a shantyboat.

We hastened the last steps of preparation and were soon on the eve of departure. Rising at daybreak next morning we made ready to get under way with that eager anticipation, never without a trace of fear at what might befall, which had so many times been the stirring prelude to a day of drifting down new reaches of the river. The date of our leaving the slip of the Harvey shipyard was May 2, 1950. Though we had been there only a little more than three weeks, the river and drifting seemed to belong to a previous existence.

When I had moved the gangplanks alongside the boat and lashed them in their accustomed places under the catwalks, then loosed the shore lines and coiled and hung them up, instead of shoving out into the current and gliding away, as we used to do, we now lined up the boats, cranked the skiff engine, and steered out into the canal.

It was an anxious moment, being the first trial of towing the shantyboat with the skiff. The initial hookup was shantyboat ahead, skiff towing from behind. Later we tried other arrangements, but this was best and became our unvarying practice. An important advantage was increased steering power and control. This we learned at once, for we were able to make a neat, sharp turn from the slip into the canal.

In all our later cruising a slower fleet than ours was never met with; yet, being accustomed to the uncertainties of drifting with the river, our new way of traveling was fast enough. The engine gave us the great advantage of being able to go and stop when we wanted to instead of having our movements controlled by the current.

Perhaps it was well to be taught at the very outset of our cruise that our schedule was to be interfered with by the fallibility of machinery, if not by natural forces. When we were only half a mile down the canal, as I was steering in the skiff and of course watching the engine—its flywheel spinning, valves lifting regularly—I noticed gasoline dripping from the carburetor. We at once worked our fleet into a side canal, fortunately at hand, and tied up. Not being able to figure out what the trouble was, I took the skiff, which ran well enough in spite of the leak, back to our helpful neighbor at the boatyard. He said there must be something wrong with the carburetor float, which had given us trouble before. We had then tried to remedy it by whittling a float out of balsa wood from a discarded life preserver. Even though shellacked, this had soaked up gasoline and become ineffective. We now made a second float of the same balsa wood and gave it several coats of shellac. When installed it worked very well, but these floats were never satisfactory. When one became too heavy I would replace it with the spare, drying out the first to use later. After a while we bought a regular cork float and had no more trouble with this detail.

Tinkering with the engine held us up for two days. The small canal in which our boats were moored was a good harbor, except in a rainy season. It was really a drainage ditch, which in that low country is likely to be very long. It had increased in depth to carry off the storm water, so that on finally reaching the canal the ditch had become so deep that its water must be pumped up into the larger stream. Thus after heavy rains our harbor would be unsafe and disagreeable; yet it contained a small pier at which an oyster boat docked—the *Flying Eagle*.

It was May 4 when we got in motion again, to the morning songs of cardinals, a prothonotary warbler, a chat and the first locust of the season. Heading south on the canal we entered the green portal of the forest.

IV

In this part of our voyage we were following the old route which connected New Orleans to the marshland, used in the earliest days of settlement by French trappers who paddled their laden pirogues up the shallow extremity of Bayou Barataria to a point not far from the Mississippi, an easier and safer route than the open, swift river afforded. The bayou was also used by Jean Lafitte and his band of pirates, who could slip into the city by this unguarded back way from their hangout in Barataria Bay. Many a cargo of contraband was poled and paddled through the swampy forest by boatmen who knew the intricate waterway so well they could keep their bateaux in the right channel even in the darkness of night. As the city grew, the commercial value of the Barataria route became apparent, and a canal to connect it directly with the Mississippi was begun by D'Estreban, the colonial landowner, using the labor of slaves with picks and shovels. After many years as a private canal, it was taken over by the United States government. A new lock and dredging to meet the Intracoastal dimensions of twelve feet deep and one hundred and twenty-five feet wide have made a modern waterway—though already inadequate—of the old canal, no trace of which survives except the name, for Col. Harvey was not an officer of the United States Engineer Division, but the son-in-law of old D'Estreban.

It would have suited us better to penetrate the swampy forest by way of a natural stream and follow its twisting way among roots of cypress and massive trunks under an arch of foliage which screened the sun; but even though the canal cut a straight swath through the forest and its banks were cleared of trees for two or three rods back, the untouched wilderness, now in the lush green of early summer, seemed as wild and primitive as it had ever been.

The novelty of seeing our boat move through the water instead of drifting with the current added to the interest of our voyage. Our senses alive to every new detail in our passage, we gazed expectantly into every opening in the trees. One of these led into a small bay encircled by the green wall, and moored there was a fleet of abandoned barges and boats, one of these being the *Amos K. Gordon*, a steam sternwheel towboat which had several times passed us when we came down the Mississippi. To see this river friend among the forlorn hulks rusting away in the depths of the forest was a pathetic sight, a reminder that all of man's works will in time disappear into the ever-flourishing wilderness.

After some miles the woods became thinner toward the south and we had glimpses of the open prairie which lies like a green band along the Gulf shore. After we had tied up for the night—having crowded the shantyboat into the entrance of a small canal called on our maps the Hero Canal—we walked a short distance inland along the solid bank of the ditch, which extended as far into the darkening marsh as we could see. The opaque water in the small canal seemed alive with garfish, and we watched the big brown fellows as they rose to the surface time after time in a swift arc, as if playing a game. It was a delightful summer evening. In the wilderness we at last came to ourselves again, as if part of us had been dormant in the city. Our voyage lay before us, a carefree, joyous adventure toward the setting sun.

In the morning the engine would not start. After some probing I found water inside the cylinder, and when this was cleaned out the engine popped off and ran well enough. I hoped the trouble was due only to a faulty gasket.

A head wind made our rate of progress so slow that we gave it up after a few miles and pulled into Hole-in-Wall Cut-off, or rather around to the back side of the small, triangular island which lay between the cut and the old bend of Bayou Barataria. It was good to be off the Intracoastal and have it clear out of sight. Our only companion here was an abandoned barge, a large wooden hull with a full cabin.

After the recent busy days of preparation and departure from Harvey, we were pleased now to relax and fall into easier shantyboat ways. I explored the old barge, which had been used as a quarterboat. The water here being clean, I had my first swim in weeks. We bathed together on the sunny deck and had some music in what remained of daylight.

When we were ready to leave, the motor could not be started until I removed the head and dried out the inside. Something must be done about this. Rather than retreat to Harvey, we decided to run farther down the bayou until near a road where I could get whatever help, repairs or parts might be required.

Once it was started the engine ran smoothly, doubtless evaporating the water as it seeped in and exhausting it as steam. By good fortune we came upon a harbor within rowing distance of the road and the first houses of the settlement. I shut off the skiff engine as soon as possible, drained the cooling system, and gave my attention to mooring the boat and settling in for an extended stay.

This point was ten miles from Harvey and we had been three days on the way. Though Morgan City seemed as distant as ever, we were not in the least discouraged. The relation between time and distance is flexible and, after all, we were as well off here as there.

Looking about our new domain we were thankful, as we have been many times, that chance had led us to this particular place and permitted us to live there briefly. Before the shantyboat, which was moored in a small loop of the old bayou, lay a pastoral shore which could have been along a river, a firm and grassy meadow where cattle grazed among clumps of willows; yet white and dark blue herons reminded us that it was a Louisiana landscape. South and east the open prairie extended to the horizon, an ocean of waving grass in which a far-off grove stood out like an island and single trees had the appearance of square-

riggers under sail. Above the flat earth the pageant of the sky rolled in all its splendor.

Next day we took possession of the shore by stringing a clothesline among the willows and hanging out a large washing. The tubs were set up on deck on the same wash bench we had carried on the roof all the way from Brent. A fire was built on shore for heating water. The bayou water had a dark appearance, like sea water, but it was only slightly brackish and a tubful of it was quite clear. The canal had been of an opaque muddiness at Harvey. For this and other reasons a washing had been impossible to achieve there, but now we let ourselves go and worked with abandon. By the day's end everything was clean and dry and stowed away.

I now gave my attention to the skiff engine, removed the cylinder head, and on careful examination found a small hole in the exhaust port. In the hope that it could be welded I decided to take it to a shop I had seen on one of my earlier visits to Barataria. The first part of this trip was by johnboat to the point where the road began. Here I changed from boat to bicycle and continued along the bayou on a road of white shells for a short distance, then on a blacktop road for some five miles. A lane turned off, and at the end of it close to the water stood a cluster of small buildings—a few houses, Fleming's Canal Store, a boatbuilder's shed, and the welder's shop. The water was wider here for it was like a crossroads—Bayou Barataria turned southward toward the Gulf, the Intracoastal continued to the west as a dug canal, and from the north came a wide channel, Bayou Willow, which was an outlet of Lake Salvador. There was so much of bayou life and activity concentrated at this point that we were to visit it often during our stay on Barataria.

The welder took one look at the old cylinder head and said no, showing me how thin the metal had been made by rust. "You must get a new part," he declared. "Maybe Carmadelle has one."

Following his directions I circled around by a bridge to the other side of the bayou, and upon entering Carmadelle's store, felt that it was within the range of possibility that any part of any engine could be found there. It was a large place but so chock full that the post office had to be accommodated in a lean-to on the side. The charm of a country store was enhanced by a stock of marine supplies—nets, net preservatives, small anchors, boat fittings, gadgets, engines, cordage, and some coarse stuff in large balls like binder twine, used for crab fishing lines.

Even with such potentialities behind him, Mr. Carmadelle could not supply me with a new cylinder head. He said he would get one on his next trip to the city, and being in no hurry I accepted his offer.

We decided to paint the skiff while it was out of service. On a high tide, by means of a block and tackle, some stray boards, and pieces of iron pipe for rollers, Anna and I were able to haul the skiff out on the low bank.

The copper paint for the bottom—made in Gloucester, Massachusetts and bearing a label designed in the days of sailing ships—was bought from the Crown Point store near our landing, for all the stores on Barataria have marine supplies, however limited their other stock may be. I had an idea of painting the upper part of the skiff white with red and blue trim, as a Cajun boat should be painted, but the matter was settled otherwise by the gift of a bucketful of gray paint from the mate of a small tug which had tied up near us.

This tug was filling a tank barge with water, a strange proceeding it seemed to us until the mate explained that they were getting fresh water for steam boilers used in the drilling of oil wells out in the Gulf. They had come up the bayou until the water tested a low enough salinity to be safely used in the boilers.

In our work on the skiff we were advised and assisted by sixteen-year-old Roy Prestonback, who had appeared soon after our arrival on this shore, sauntering through the willow grove with his gun and dog. He came aboard our "campboat" without hesitation, perfectly at ease, and stayed a long time—for dinner, in fact, conversing on many topics with wit and good sense. He was already experienced in the world, locally, and told us entertaining and informative yarns of his cruise out into the bay as a hand on a trawler. According to our notions Roy was mature and capable beyond his years, but we were to learn that he was no exception among Cajun children.

The Prestonbacks were our nearest neighbors, living in a barren cottage on the open bayou shore, so close to the water that we passed their door on our way to Crown Point in the skiff or johnboat. The Prestonbacks must always use a boat to go anywhere, too, because the road was cut off by a side canal before it reached their house. With their German name the Prestonbacks could not have been Acadian originally, but they were now as French as the next, the first one to arrive here having doubtless married a French girl, as had all his descendants.

There were seven Prestonback children—a moderate-sized family in Louisiana—of whom Roy was the oldest. The father was away working, but Mrs. Prestonback and the children came to visit us one day, arriving in their skiff, all of them happy, lively, and friendly. The only frequent visitors, however, were Roy and the next in line, Chester, who had introduced himself by showing us his seven-toed foot.

We enjoyed the company of these boys and learned much from them. They were the best instructors we could have had in the nature and customs of this strange land. The boys in turn were curious about Kentucky. I gave them some black walnuts, which they tried to crack with their teeth, like pecans; and groundhogs were unheard-of animals. The boys liked to eat dinner with us. When Anna served pokeweed, which they had never considered as food, Roy called it grass but ate it with relish. He particularly liked Anna's whole-wheat biscuits, or, as he preferred to call them, "cakes." With some black walnuts, orange peel, or sunflower seeds added to them, it is no wonder Roy and Chester came so often at mealtime. We have often observed that the flavor of pure whole-grain bread made of freshly-ground flour appeals to every taste except the most prejudiced. Its goodness often comes as a revelation.

We were enjoying wheat again, having been able to buy some in New Orleans. But hen scratch had served us well, and we would grind our flour of it again before leaving that country in which no wheat is grown or used.

The boys introduced us to some native foods which were new to us. Roy showed me how to find turtle eggs. Even though the elevation of this ground was a matter of inches, it was high enough above the surrounding marsh to attract the nesting turtles. Sometimes, with Skipper's help, we caught a big snapper, whose varied meat is delicious. One large turtle contained twenty-one hard-shell eggs, which of course we used. Anna baked a cake with some of them.

It was Chester who proudly showed us how to catch soft-shell crabs. He said we must hang a certain kind of green bush under water; when you pull it up, it will have a crab in it. This sounded fantastic to us but it worked. It seems that the crab casts its shell once a year in its cycle of growth, and for a few days, until the new shell hardens, the crab is defenseless, during which time it crawls into whatever protection it can find—a fisherman's bush if one is handy. We liked this primitive fishing without hook or bait. Following Chester's instructions still further, we removed the eyes and certain internals and fried the whole thing in butter, claws and all. Soft-shell crabs are rare food.

Hard-shell crabs are also easy to catch. All it takes is a piece of fresh meat tied on a string. When this is lowered into the water the crab grabs it with his claws and holds on until raised nearly to the surface where you take him with a quick dip of a net. Getting fresh meat for bait was a problem until we thought of using moccasin, cutting a snake into several pieces. This practice horrified Roy, who expected us to be poisoned.

The crabs are steamed and then comes the tedious work of extracting the meat. It comes out in shreds from the different parts of the shell and from the claws, which must be cracked open. When we first tried it the meat seemed not worth the trouble, but in time we became more expert, though never approaching the deftness of the nimble-fingered Cajun girls.

Another wild food we were enjoying in quantity was blackberries. The bushes scattered about the meadow we left for the boys to pick and went back to the island at Hole-in-Wall, where we had discovered a large brier patch. It was a snaky jungle, but paths were soon beaten down and we picked many quarts of berries there—enough for canning. These berries were of fine quality, sweet and small-seeded, a sort of cross between blackberry and dewberry.

The jars of berries were a valuable addition to the dwindling supply of canned stuff in the hold of the boat. Our stock consisted mostly of surplus from the bountiful harvest on the Cumberland River two years before. The garden crops of the last summer at Natchez were too slim to allow any for canning, but of the abundance of sweet potatoes grown there some still remained and they were good to the last. The hold was apparently an ideal place for their storage.

We had not been long at this station before we discovered the overwhelming power of Louisiana mosquitoes. They were not to be seen during the daylight—in all our stay in this country neither mosquitoes nor flies bothered us by day—but at nightfall they descended in clouds. Our little boat was the focal point for all the insects of miles of prairie and swamp. The dogs soon learned of this menace and were glad to come inside and stay there. After dark no door was opened, no lamp lighted. Though all cracks in the cabin were stopped up, the mosquitoes still found a way in—until at length Anna discovered their entrance down through the roof around the chimney. When this hole was closed we slept in peace under a sort of tent made of netting suspended over the bed, the old-fashioned mosquito bar.

Now we understood why the Cajun houses had solid wood shutters to all doors and windows. During the day Mrs. Prestonback's door stood open and there were no screens, but at night all was closed up.

We regretted that the balmy nights must be spent indoors, and envied the frogs out in the fresh coolness. Such croaking had never been heard. Sometimes it was like the bleating of lambs or the grunting of pigs, or we could imagine the uproar to be a percussion orchestra of savages. The noise would rise to a frenzied pitch, then break off suddenly, only to begin again after a few seconds of silence in another spot as if coming from antiphonal choirs, or as if different bands were competing.

Each night we watched the bright gleaming of the lightning bugs. Never were they as numerous, as brilliant, as slow-moving and languorous. They settled in one particular clump of tall grass outside our window and, motionless, flashed their lights on and off until the grass was radiant with sparkles, and all so quiet.

On one of these nights Skipper had a long-expected litter of pups, the eighth of the voyage as we calculated. The evening had been troublesome to her and to us. She insisted on getting into the clothes closet or into our bed, anywhere except into the box of torn newspaper we had prepared for her. It was a general relief when she decided to go outside, where she made a nest in the grass. All went well in spite of blood-sucking insects, and there were seven pups, one more than usual—two black, two brown, two white with brown spots, and one like Skipper, white with black spots. With such diversity it was easier to understand how she had produced Sambo, who was solid black, long-haired, and a monster compared with his terrierlike mother.

One day we saw in the Crown Point store a handbill announcing the Annual Pirogue Race on Bayou Barataria. We asked Roy about this and his animated description made it an event we wanted to see. The race was to be on a Sunday afternoon. During the morning of that day motorboats of all types, from outboards to yachts, passed westward on the canal, many of them coming from New Orleans. We joined the procession in our newly-painted skiff, stopping to pick up Roy at his house.

Farther along we made another stop at a waterside cemetery where Roy said Indian relics could be found. The graves were on a low ridge of shells—the "shell pile" frequently found in the marshes. We never learned for sure how these shell piles originated, but Roy's explanation was that Indians, camping there long ago, had eaten clams and left the shells. Small fragments of Indian pottery, some crudely decorated, could be found. Of more interest to us was one of the gravestones bearing the names of Bakewell and Berthoud, a combination which suggested the family of Lucy Audubon.

The course of the race was on the lower section of Bayou Barataria, ending at the point where it widened at the junction of Bayou Willow, in front of the Canal Store. In previous races the four-and-a-half-mile distance had been covered in less than half an hour. We examined some of the racing pirogues. Much like a kayak, though undecked, they were long, light, and so narrow that even the practiced Cajun had to watch his balance. He paddled with a single-bladed paddle, always on one side, the stern of the pirogue having a slight twist in it to keep the boat on a straight course. I had an idea that a double-bladed paddle might be faster.

We chose to see the finish of the race and found a place for our skiff among the assembled fleet of motorboats which lined the whole course. Besides pleasure boats, there were others belonging to the oil companies, a Coast Guard cutter, boats with news photographers and race officials, and, of course, native skiffs and pirogues.

It was not long before the word was passed, "Here they come!" and the winning racer appeared. Other pirogues came in sight, singly and in groups, but still they came, the leaders being trailed by a fleet of common, everyday pirogues paddled by young men and boys in work clothes who had no chance of winning. We understood then what Roy had meant by saying that everyone to finish the race would get a prize. The prizes were distributed from a stand erected in a grove of live oaks at the waterside. A large crowd gathered there after the race and many picnics were soon spread out on the grass. Anna and I wandered among the noisy, jovial crowd, feeling lonely and far away. We recovered Roy, who had all the while been entertained—or did he do the entertaining?—aboard a New Orleans motorboat, and made for home.

After remaining at this station near Crown Point for the greater part of May, we decided to move down Bayou Barataria to that section where the pirogue race had been held, in order to be closer to the Cajun houses and fishing boats. Getting away was not so easy. We had entered this cove on a high tide and now our boat was fast aground. The Gulf tides are of small range—otherwise such a low, flat land could never have been formed—and at our distance inland the variation in water level is due mostly to continued wind from north or south. Unless we waited for another high tide, the only chance of getting our boat into deeper water lay in taking advantage of the swell caused by the passing of a large tug hauling loaded barges. We had noticed that such a tow moving at a fair rate of speed would first suck all the water away, leaving us sitting in the mud; then the water would rush back to a level above normal. This surge might be enough to float our boat, and if we heaved at just the right moment we might be able to get off the mud flat. To this end we ran a line out to a piling at the edge of the canal and waited.

The boats that went by on the morning of our intended departure were either too small to cause a swell, or considerably slowed down when near us. Then one came from the New Orleans direction which looked promising—not a tug but a large white craft like a yacht. To our disappointment it, too, slowed down—in fact, came to a dead stop. We saw it was a Coast Guard cutter. An officer with a megaphone shouted a question which I made out to be, "Have you had your census taken yet?"

"No!" I yelled back.

"Did you say 'No'?"

"Yes!"

To clear up the matter I put out to them in our johnboat, with Sambo who was always one jump ahead of me. Climbing over the rail while a crewman kept the johnboat from scraping their paint and Sambo from trying to follow me, I found the census taker seated at a table on deck. He was almost as new at this game as I was, ours probably being the first campboat he had met coming out of New Orleans; and I don't think he could have found a more puzzling case than ours. There seemed to be no classification for people living on boats. The best we could do for our home was to call it a one-room dwelling unit, detached and not dilapidated. Central heat? No method of keeping warm could be more central than a fireplace. Running water? No, yet we lived in running water. Bathtub? No, but we took a bath every day, often in the running water. Inside toilet? Yes. How could that be without running water? Well, perhaps it was an outside one inside. Electricity? No; no radio, no television, no conveniences whatever.

When it came to employment, I explained that I was an artist; so the man listed me as self-employed. "How many hours did you work last week?" I named a figure at random; we must get through with this somehow. "Last year, in how many weeks did you do any work at all, not counting work around the house?" Even a lengthy explanation might not answer this question. Some say an artist works all the time, others that he never works. Except for some sketching, all my work as an artist was done at home where it was hopelessly mixed up with many other pursuits.

I was even more at a loss when the question of income was put to me. The census taker tried to help. "Two thousand dollars a year?" I thought he was joking.

"How about one thousand?"

"No," I insisted.

"Well, five hundred dollars?" I let it go at that, with a guilty feeling. How many years was it since I had sold that picture for seventy-five dollars?

It was a relief to both of us when the last answer was written down. The cutter moved on down the canal to look for other prospects, and I rowed back to our substandard home to tell Anna all about it.

It was not long before the tug *Aztec* came by with some loaded barges at a speed that washed us out of the mud. We hooked up the skiff and proceeded down Bayou Barataria. As we sailed along that sunny afternoon the bayou and its shores seemed more fair than I remembered them from my earlier trips by land. The best way to see any stream or shore is from the deck of a boat—your own boat, if possible, and traveling at your own pace.

In this flat country all the bridges that span the bayou are down so close to the water that only a skiff or pirogue can slip under them. It was on this afternoon's run that we came to the first of the many bridges, no two of them alike, that would be opened for us to pass through. The procedure is to blow three blasts on your horn or whistle—ours was the tin foghorn which Anna still called the fish horn. If the bridge is mechanically operated, as most of the highway bridges are, it has a siren which will sound three times when the bridge is to be opened, as a warning to traffic on the road. This is a common Louisiana sound, and the numerous bridges heighten the interest of bayou navigation. In more remote sections the old bridges are picturesque wooden structures from which one never knows what to expect when he sounds his horn.

A short run took us to that part of Bayou Barataria beyond the Intracoastal route, and here we sought a harbor for our campboat, not easy to find among the private slips and landings. When I asked a fisherman, he said that the island between Bay-

ous Barataria and Willow, where the Intracoastal cut across, would not do because of our dogs—a man was raising some kind of fur-bearing rats there, which we later learned were nutria. This fisherman suggested a small canal out on Bayou Willow, farther from the settlement than we had intended to be, but it seemed best to go there. We reached this harbor in time to see the sunset fade over the surrounding marsh, which was open as the sky. One forgets the welcome the wilderness can give; it is like coming home.

The vast emptiness around us was exciting. Two or three poles stuck in the muddy bottom by some fisherman were objects to which the eye and mind continually returned. In the level plane of earth and water, the few scrubby trees at the canal mouth were friendly and reassuring. On the open and solid shore was a low roof supported by four poles, "t'ached," as Roy would say, with palmetto fronds. This and other signs of continued and recent occupation gave the place the character of an established landing. We learned later that the last inhabitant there had killed himself.

In the trees lived an orchard oriole, a bird whose pleasant song can be heard in many an outpost in the marsh. In this diminutive grove were also a chat and a Carolina wren, and we heard a cardinal, chickadee, and Maryland yellowthroat among the chorus of infinite redwings. There was a poignancy to the songs of these birds associated with woods and hills.

Bayou Willow, called Bayou Vilars on our charts, would have made a wide river. It was one of the outlets of the large, shallow Lake Salvador a mile farther north. This lake was the fishing ground of the many passing skiffs, some fast as speedboats—an ill-considered use of power, we thought; yet some of them might be going far enough to make the speed worthwhile. A few of the fishermen were after soft-shell crabs, and boatloads of bushes went by, old brown ones being moved from one spot to another, and freshly cut green ones.

The daily trips of a big crew boat belonging to an oil company were a nuisance, its high waves rolling into the shallow water in which we lay. On one occasion we were so tossed about that our copper boiler full of rain water was lost from the afterdeck. Had this powerful boat met us when we were traveling, it would have slowed down.

A crab fisherman often put out his lines near us. He was a dark-skinned, wizened Cajun whose speech we could hardly understand. We never did comprehend the name he gave to our side canal. His long crab lines were baited with chunks of cow lip, so tough that even a crab could not devour it, tied to the line at three- or four-foot intervals. He traced the lines while kneeling in the bow of his tiny skiff, and when a crab appeared, holding to the bait, he expertly flipped it into the boat by means of a small, shallow dip net. Some crab fishermen ran their engine at slow speed while tracing their long lines, which passed over a spool extending from the side of the boat. We became friendly with this fisherman at Bayou Willow. In a shy way he encouraged us to stay there, and seeing our interest in catching soft-shells told us how easy it was to make a good living in that manner with little equipment. He also told me I was using the wrong kind of bush. This was not Chester's fault, but there are two bushes quite alike and here I had gotten hold of the wrong one. What difference it makes to the crab I do not know.

Looking southward from our harbor, all we could see of Barataria was a dark mass of trees showing a few flecks of houses and boats. On our first trip there the skiff engine suddenly overheated and I found the circulation of the cooling system was stopped. The valve to keep the water from draining out when the engine ceased running was simply a metal ball. This had been worn so small by long use that it stuck in the opening. Luckily Carmadelle had a new ball in stock. After this experience we constantly watched the exhaust, into which the cooling system overflowed. If there was no steam, the cooling system was not functioning.

We made several runs down the bayou and found much to interest us on water and shores. Beyond the point where the

Intracoastal leaves the bayou, Barataria becomes even more picturesque and intimate. It is like a village street, with much local traffic in pirogues and skiffs. Both shores are built up, in a modest way, and one sees small stores, workshops, and boatyards here and there. Every place has its own dock and boats. The doctor's shingle faces the bayou above his own landing, and he no doubt makes some of his calls by water. We liked to watch the boat builders, and looked up the shop of Adam Dufresne, the maker of our skiff, which he remembered well. This man still works without power and machinery. At a larger place trawlers were being built. One of them, forty-six feet long, had a keel of yellow pine, and another sixty-foot keel timber of fir lay nearby. Cypress is still used for planking but is becoming scarce and poor in quality even in Louisiana. Pirogues can no longer be made by hollowing out a single log. The pirogue maker we saw was constructing them of thin boards.

There were fish and crab docks along the bayou, at some of them the unique sign "Slow Down, Crab Cars" illuminated at night and intended to prevent wave damage by passing boats to the large slat crates, like live boxes, in which the soft-shelled crabs are kept. The cars can be raised out of the water by a rude windlass to allow inspection of the crabs, which are in different stages of the shedding process. Some, called busters in English, are caught just when the old shell begins to crack and are kept until the shell is gone, at which point they must be removed from the box. In our ignorance we had tried to keep some soft-shelled crabs in a fish box, but we soon did not have any soft-shells—the first ones to get hard shells had eaten the unfortunate ones which were still soft. The growing of new shells is interrupted if the crab is removed from water, but the delicate soft-shells must be handled carefully and at just the right time. Like all kinds of fishing, this is an art which requires skill, experience and natural aptitude.

With so much to see there, so much material for painting and writing, Barataria might have detained us indefinitely; yet we were travelers, and after two weeks on Bayou Willow we gave way to the desire to see new places, suddenly gathered up our traps, and sailed westward.

V

Our mechanical navigation of the canal, while prosaic compared with free drifting on the river's current, afforded delights we had not anticipated. It was pleasant to sit on the main deck in the shade and glide slowly through space and time with the smooth and gentle motion that only a boat in water can give. The sunny shores passed at a footpace. We could examine the varied grasses and plants which fringed the water—what a contrast between the elephant's-ear, with its broad, triangular leaves, and the soaring reeds—or look into the depths of the green, swampy forest hung with moss, or watch an approaching tug loom from a mere spot in the blue distance. If nothing attracted our attention we gazed with contentment down the long, empty canal which narrowed until it was lost in the infinity of space.

Skipper and Sambo, old voyagers as they were, waited patiently from one landing to the next. When drifting on the rivers they had passed much of the time sleeping, unless they happened to see a channel buoy, which they barked at as something alive; and it did look like an aquatic animal thrashing its way up the river. On the canal, however, with the shores always close, the dogs slept little lest they miss something. At sight of a muskrat or rabbit they dove from the deck of the moving boat and swam ashore for a chase. The boat's rate of speed was so slow that I could go off in the johnboat, pick up the dogs, and overtake the shantyboat before it had gone very far.

The chunking of the skiff engine behind us was a reassuring sound which went with us always. After a while only our subconscious mind listened to it, yet both of us heard instantly the slightest variation of pitch and rhythm. No vibration from the engine could be felt on deck, a fact which added to our pleasure. In the beginning one of us had to sit in the skiff and steer, looking ahead through the two open doors of the cabin, but by this time I had rigged tiller lines from the skiff along each side of the shantyboat, and the steersman could enjoy the comfort of the main deck.

Other fine points had been worked out by experiment. For instance, if the skiff were lashed in a direct line with the shantyboat it would not hold a straight course, probably due to the thrust of the propeller. I found that when the skiff was lashed at just the correct angle, little steering was necessary. The skiff was held in position by two diagonal lines from its stern to the corners of the shantyboat's afterdeck, so that by adjusting these lines it was easy to hold the skiff in the proper position. The johnboat was tied to one of the corners of the afterdeck, allowing it to trail along parallel to the skiff.

Navigation on the canal was much less hazardous than drifting on the wide, swift river, yet we had to be vigilant and careful even on the placid Intracoastal, since no kind of boating is without some danger. The narrowness of the canal, while preventing wind waves, did not allow much leeway in passing a tug. The pilots almost without exception slowed down when near us, but the greatest danger was beyond their control. A big tug often pulled five barges in a line, and if these barges were empty a cross wind would swing them to one side so that the last barge raked the shore, making a trap from which no small boat could escape. We always calculated on this and passed to windward. If our course seemed to be taking us to a point where two tugs would pass each other, we tied up to the shore so as to let them get by us one at a time. We made it a rule never to stop along the canal bank unless we could get under way instantly. For all our caution, we were later to make one mistake in judgment which nearly cost us our boats.

We felt like experienced boatmen when we left Bayous Willow and Barataria with Bayou Lafourche as our next objective. This was one of the sections of the Intracoastal, each dug through the marsh, apparently laid out with a ruler into long reaches extending in a certain direction for a mile, five miles, ten; then, shifting a few degrees as if correcting its course, it makes another straight run on this new bearing.

Though not expecting much from these purely artificial sections of the Intracoastal, we found they had a charm and character of their own. They took us through a land which would otherwise have been impenetrable; and though the landscape is of elemental simplicity, which is its grandest feature, it offers such continuous change and variation, though all within a narrow range, that the senses and imagination of the voyager are kept ever alert.

On this section west from Barataria, where the long canal lay ahead of us like a gleaming furrow, we first noticed the striking contrast between the two shores. The side toward which the furrow had been turned, that is, the side on which the spoil from dredging had been piled, being somewhat higher had attracted a riverbank vegetation—willows, even cottonwoods, and a thick growth of vines and bushes, blackberries, pokeweed, wild grape and elderberries, now white masses of bloom. On the other side was the primeval marsh, a golden plain fringed with dark green elephant's-ear plants along the water and extending to the horizon, with dark patches of cloud shadow and far-off lakes and bayous gleaming in the sun.

Although the distance from Barataria to Lafourche is only twenty miles, with nothing between but grass, trees and water, we made extended stops at three places along the way.

The first was at Bayou Perot. Only a few miles from Barataria, its name had never been mentioned, and we were surprised to find the bayou as wide as a good-sized river, though perhaps its low shores make it seem wider than it is. The wild desolation of Bayou Perot attracted us and we looked about for a solid shore at which to land—for the benefit of the dogs, whose requirements in this respect it is best to heed, a lesson we had learned long ago. For ourselves it would often have been a pleasure to anchor offshore, since after all we had a boat, not a house, and we could be independent of land.

Seeing no harbor for us, we steered down Bayou Perot a short distance to be out of the way of Intracoastal traffic, and moored our boat—not by dropping the anchor, our faithful standby on the river, but by sticking a long pole in the muddy bottom and making fast to that. A pole or two for this purpose we always kept handy, and another for turning or moving the boat—this one being copied after those seen on fishing boats, with two blunt horns on the end forming a rude trident which gave more bearing in the bottomless ooze.

There was a lone fisherman out on the wide Bayou Perot tracing a trot line from a pirogue, his skiff moored to the float which located his line. I rowed out to him and had a friendly talk. He pointed out a small side canal on the far shore which we found had been dug in drilling an oil well—all oil drilling in the marsh is done from barges, and canals are dug to the chosen spot just as roads would be made in a firm land. This well had turned out to be a dry one—dry, at least, of oil—and the abandoned casing still remained in the water at the end of the short canal. Here, as along the Intracoastal, the spoil from dredging made a firm shore on one side where we could walk on dry land, and where Skipper and Sambo chased rabbits up and down until they escaped into the marsh. The swamp rabbits are large and good to eat.

The next day we went up the bayou half a mile in the skiff to see Lake Salvador. It seemed an immense body of water when we sailed into it. The low shore on the other side could not be seen except for some wooded parts which stood out like separate islands. The wildness of the scene was not lessened by the willow poles of fishermen sticking up everywhere—they might have been left by savages; nor by an oil rig standing far out in the water, a mystic structure with a fiery torch. The water was smooth as glass, though a storm had just passed to westward where the setting sun was breaking through with great spokes of light and color.

Bayou Perot was marked by a flashing beacon; necessary, too, for we could not make out the entrance from the lake when we turned around. On the way back we stopped at an extensive shell pile along the bayou. Here grew some great live oaks, and under them was a group of small cabins occupied only during the trapping season, untenanted now except for an old man, the fisherman had told us, and a dog. A slight dock extended out into the shallow water, and its plank walk continued as the main thoroughfare of the miniature village, winding among the trunks of the grotesque oaks, crossing ditches and leading past all the neat houses, some of which had small galleries and even curtained windows. It was pleasant to hear the cardinal and Carolina wren among the trees and to look out from the shady grove onto the sunny prairie. We tried to imagine what this place was like during the busy season, all the cabins occupied, the sound of French and the smell of Cajun cooking in the air; but not even the old man was to be seen this day.

A spreading fig tree was loaded with fruit, not yet ripe unfortunately except for a few around the edge. As we were leaving, the resident dog appeared and tried to jump into our boat. He landed in the water and Sambo jumped in after him. It was a fierce engagement until I managed to hoist Sambo inboard and put off.

On these skiff excursions we were protected from the June sun by a small awning stretched between two poles, such as a Chinese fisherman would have over his little boat. On board the shantyboat we minded the heat only during times of dead calm. A steady breeze and frequent showers go to make the bayou summer tolerable in spite of the blazing sun. The little pups suffered from the heat through the day, and though we put them in the coolest place, they lay stretched on their bellies, panting and whimpering. To us the heat became oppressive at nightfall when we went to bed and shrouded ourselves with the mosquito bar. The air always cooled off during the night, however, and mornings were delightful. Dawn seemed unusually quiet, the cacophony of insects and frogs having ceased, and its freshness lasted well into the mornings.

The solitary fisherman was the only person we saw during our stay at Bayou Perot. I would row out when he came to trace the line nearest us, for he was a good man to talk to. His home was in Barataria, but he liked Bayou Perot and often passed the night in a tar-paper shack near the shell-pile cabins. Fishing was best in the fall of the year, he said, but that did not stay his interest or zeal. His lines were much like Ohio River trot lines, but with some refinements, such as small swivels on the staging so the fish could not twist themselves off, and floats to keep the line above the bottom. He took off some nice ones while I watched, catfish which might have come from the Mississippi. The yellow cats he called *goujons*. The smaller fish were carefully measured since the undersized ones could not be sold. Some of these he saved for us, and most welcome they were.

We set out the bushes we had carried with us and caught so many soft-shelled crabs that the dogs had to help eat them. Following the fisherman's advice we made a trip to the lake for clams, which could be picked up from the muddy bottom at an arm's depth. Returning, we visited the trappers' village again to get drinking water from one of the above-ground cisterns of wood. As we picked some half-ripe figs we thought how pleasant it would be to stay there, to wait for the figs to ripen and for the long summer to pass.

A few days later, however, we were cruising in the early morning down the straight canal, watching the boats approach and recede, listening to the two choirs of birds—the cardinal, towhee, chat, Maryland yellowthroat, kingbird, and Carolina wren on the willow side, and in the marsh numberless redwings, whose continuo was interrupted by the raucous boat-tailed grackles.

Our next stop was made in a narrower canal on the right called on our charts Harvey Canal No. 2. It served to connect the Intracoastal with the western end of Lake Salvador, whose length is nearly fourteen miles. In earlier days, before the Intracoastal was dug, this old canal and Lake Salvador were part of the water route from New Orleans westward, a winding, shallow channel which accommodated only small boats and barges.

We thought that our shantyboat would be out of the way of traffic in this side canal, but on the first night the *Mary-Joan* passed toward the lake, returning shortly with a barge of shells. There seemed to be no place to which the *Mary-Joan* did not go. It had passed us at Harvey and Barataria, and we were to see it many times on narrow bayous to the west, usually towing a shell barge or two. This gas-driven stern-wheeler made us a little homesick, for it was like so many we used to see on the Ohio River before the days of barge line monopolies. Surely the *Mary-Joan* had been designed by a riverman from the Ohio, and built by him, too, for it had the slightly homemade look of the *B.D. Raike* or the *Juanita*. The *Mary-Joan* made a clanking noise that we could always recognize from afar. As it passed we waved and were greeted in return by the pilot, the crew, the womenfolk and assorted boys and girls.

The shores of Harvey Canal No. 2 were a little higher and showed a marked difference from the lowlands of Bayou Perot. Cattle grazed in the willow woods, and I found blackberries and poke for us to pick. Walking about on dry ground again was a rare pleasure, as it had been on the Lower Ohio when the river fell after the flood.

Some crab fishermen, Bayou Lafourche men, passed us on their way to and from the lake, and they stopped to talk. One of them mentioned a good campboat harbor just before you reach the town of Larose, which is at the junction of the Intracoastal and Lafourche. We at once moved on to this place, which was a small cove along the Intracoastal with firm and grassy shores bordered by tall willows. A sign on a tree said Keep Out, but since our friend had advised us to pay no attention to it, we forced our way through a mat of hyacinths and tied up. There was evidence that another campboat had been here for a long time, and had left but recently.

The outfit which had been here before us now lay in a branch canal not far off. I talked with the owner and learned that he was from the Atchafalaya River at Morgan City. His boat looked like a river shantyboat—they have their own marks, and their design is different from the bayou campboat, being more seaworthy, with a deeper hull, more freeboard, and easy rakes. The campboat, never in strong current or rough water, is more house and less boat. Many have overhangs at the ends, a higher roof, often with a ridge, and the decks are close to the water.

This man said he could make the run to Morgan City within a day; perhaps he could with his pushboat, more powerful than ours, of which he was somewhat scornful. For us Morgan City was still so far off that we hadn't begun to calculate how long it would take us to get there.

We saw other fishermen from Morgan City trying their luck in this section of the canal, and also local men and boys—yes, and women, too, for one lady went along in the skiff when her husband ran his lines. They used small shad for bait, sometimes catching them from a moving skiff with a tapering net made of fine wire, but more often with a cast net. It was here we had our first good look at a cast net and saw how it was handled. It is flat, circular, perhaps nine feet in diameter, of fine thread and small mesh. Around the circumference, spaced about two inches apart, are balls of lead. A number of strings called brails run from the outside to the center, where they pass through a metal ring to be joined in a single string. The trick of casting the net is to make it land on the water flat and outspread. The lead weights quickly sink the net, but the caster has kept hold of the single line, which makes a pocket of the net by drawing in the brails.

The fisherman standing in the bow of his skiff gracefully casts his net time after time with a swinging motion as rhythmic as mowing with a scythe or as cradling grain—cast flat, draw up puckered, turn and empty in the boat, cast again. The boat is kept moving slowly by the current, the breeze, or the pulling in of the net. An adept Cajun can throw a cast net while standing in a pirogue, an act of delicate balance which we did not believe possible until we saw it done.

Some of the fishermen used hoop nets like those on the Mississippi River, made of heavy tarred twine, nine or ten feet long with seven hoops and two throats inside, being four feet in diameter at the open end and diminishing to a point. On the river the net is kept stretched out by the current, open and downstream. In the sluggish bayous and canals it is extended between two stakes. The stakes must be short lest they be clipped by boat propellers, and setting them in eight or ten feet of water is a neat trick. The fisherman uses a long pole which has a piece of iron pipe on the end. The stake to which the net is attached is placed in the hollow of the pipe with its point extending and then rammed into the muddy bottom; the pole is withdrawn, leaving the stake.

Catfish were still the prime fish, bringing the best price, but goo and buffalow were caught in quantity. The goo is the same fish we called perch on the Ohio River, drumfish in the Tennessee district of the Mississippi. The Cajun name, it is said, is short for *gaspergou*.

Garfish are a nuisance to the fisherman because they often cut their way out of his nets. It was here I caught the biggest spike-nosed gar we ever saw, in a small net made of chicken wire. Even an undersized gar is a mean fish to clean. A strip must be hacked off of its back with a hatchet from tail to head; then the armored hide can be peeled off in a sheet with a knife. After we had cleaned and cooked as much of this big one as we and the dogs could eat, I dragged the carcass far into the woods. Soon buzzards began to circle overhead, increasing until there were at least fifty, though not a one had been seen for days before. Skipper considered the gar as her property and fought off the buzzards, who settled just out of reach in low branches to wait their chance.

Some turtles were caught, green striped ones with small heads, a kind considered inedible, even poisonous, up the Mississippi. A young Lafourche fisherman named Bourg, calling them by a French name we did not understand, told us they were good to eat. We took his word for it and found they were excellent.

Soon after our arrival here we went in the skiff to Larose, two miles ahead. The dogs were left at home but they followed, running along the shore and swimming the ditches until they caught up with us and we took them in. Larose is a puzzling, formless town, strung along north and south on each side of Bayou Lafourche, and cut through the middle, east and west, by the Intracoastal, the four sections being loosely held together by three bridges and a ferry.

To approach a strange town by water gives the place a unique interest never felt by a traveler passing through it on the highway, which tends to make all places alike. Larose became another port of call for us. We landed and sauntered about the streets, feeling quite apart from the dwellers on land, yet keenly interested in all we saw and heard. The dogs were busy with their own affairs, but there was no danger of losing them. It was almost impossible to keep them out of stores, for even if we went in and left them outside, they would slip through the door with the next customer. Sambo was persistent. After we had managed to get into the post office without him, we heard the postmaster suddenly ask the clerk with some alarm, "Whose big black dog is this, anyway?" Sambo, not content to wait for us at the front door with Skipper, had circled around the building and come in by the back way. Skipper was the one to attract attention in Mr. Duco's grocery store. He thought she was such a fine dog that he offered to take the last one of her current litter of pups.

In Larose we called at the neat white cottage near the Intracoastal which was the home of Mr. Estay, one of the crab fishermen we had met while in Harvey Canal No. 2. It was a pleasure to meet jolly Mrs. Estay and those of their ten children who were at home.

Mrs. Estay's English was limited, her French voluble. Anna, an excellent French scholar, had looked forward to conversing with the Cajuns in their language, but when she tried it with Mrs. Estay the attempt was a failure. Though Anna listened and watched with intense concentration, she understood only a word now and then, some brief and plain utterance like Mrs. Estay's command to the dog, *"Passe en arrière!"* On the other hand Anna's conventional French was not recognized by the Cajun people except in a limited way.

Still, the two ladies managed to hold a lively conversation. Anna, ever keen about new foods and ways of cooking, was pleased to go into Mrs. Estay's kitchen, as neat and modern as could be, to see and smell the cooking and peep into the freezer at the pile of crab meat. Meanwhile I talked with Mr. Estay about boats and fishing. We could not have felt more at home in Kentucky or Michigan.

As we sat on the shady lawn with those friendly people, Anna and I realized that our shantyboat life was rather lonely, apart from the world and comparatively rough, with the unkempt shore for a yard; but once we had reached the boat again, we were so glad to be there that we asked no questions. This was home; it was right and natural, and we wanted nothing more.

There were more water hyacinths on this section of the Intracoastal than we had ever seen before. This plant, which has become more than a nuisance in southern waters, had been occasionally seen on the Mississippi River, even as far up as Natchez. I had to ask what it was, and was told that scattered plants are carried into the river by tows coming out of the Intracoastal. The hyacinth cannot survive in the cold, swift waters of the Mississippi, but in the quiet bayous and canals, where ice is almost unknown, it flourishes unchecked, except on waterways where traffic is heavy or where government control is practiced. We were grieved to see many small canals and inviting bayous closed to us by an unbroken green mat.

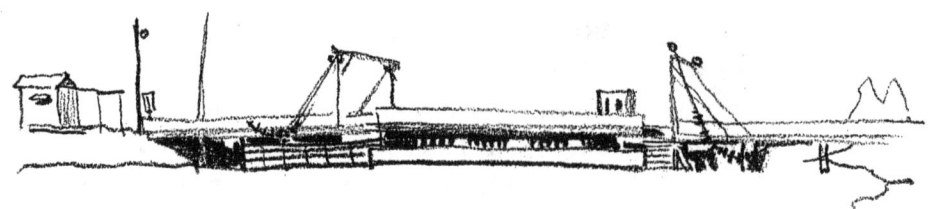

The hyacinth drifts on the water unattached, kept afloat by its bladderlike stem. It is a beautiful plant, of a fresh dark green color, with leaves something like those of the skunk cabbage, and it has pinkish lavender flowers. The charms of the "lily" fade, however, after even a short acquaintance. It gathers into green rafts which reminded us of ice floes on the Ohio River. Like the ice, it hinders all navigation and packs around the head of the boat in such quantities that it must be poled out. To its further disgrace the hyacinth has a vile smell when stirred up or removed from the water.

The inexhaustible source of the hyacinths in our cove was a narrow canal, the outfall of a swampy forest, from which the passing boats sucked them out in great quantities. I thought to keep our harbor open by making a boom across the canal to hold back the lilies, but the first time a heavy tow went by, the mass of plants jammed against the boom with such weight that they broke through and filled the cove again. I gave it up.

The suction of boats was extremely powerful at this point. Once we found ourselves adrift, our mooring lines having snapped one after another under the strain of outrushing water.

Though the dangers are different from those on the river, where swift current, heavy drift, ice, caving banks, falling trees, bridge piers, and many other hazards must be contended with, a shantyboater can never be entirely safe in the Intracoastal, where powerful, deep-draft tows run so close to him.

The Intracoastal is like a highway, and we were beginning to long for a peaceful country road. As a change for the better, while waiting for answers to our letters and forwarded mail to arrive at Larose, we moved our fleet to Bayou Lafourche and tied up along the shore at the north edge of town, just beyond a cable ferry which was used for transporting children to the school on the east bank. Here a protected harbor was not necessary, since only fishing boats and small tugs used the bayou.

We felt at once how different Bayou Lafourche was from the canal, and from Bayous Barataria and Perot. It had the feel of a river; we seemed to be looking upstream around a river bend, and our boat was down under a bank, screened from the country beyond by willows, grapevines, and other riverbank growth. Then the thought came to us—Bayou Lafourche *is* a river, or it was until the engineers tampered with the natural system. At one time Bayou Lafourche flowed out of the Mississippi River, branching off at Donaldsonville—hence *la fourche*, the fork. Like the Mississippi in miniature, the bayou is on a ridge which is highest along the shores, sloping on each side to the swamps which parallel the bayou a mile back.

It was a populated country compared with Bayou Perot, and we were made conscious of the nearness of people in many ways—the sound of traffic on the road which ran along each side of the bayou; the splashing and voices of children swimming, cows mooing, lights at night; and in the morning chorus of birds, the crowing of roosters was mingled with songs of familiar countryside birds like the mockingbird and bobwhite. The very air was different; it was dusty and we could smell the farms and fields. We thought of Bayou Perot with some regret, remembering its emptiness and simplicity, its comforting quietness.

Meanwhile, like good travelers, we made the most of Lafourche. It was pleasant to be in farmland again and to walk along a country road. A frequent restriction of shantyboat life is the impossibility of carefree walking—one must watch every step in clambering about on uneven, obstructed shores, and never go out at night except with a lantern on some necessary errand.

In the times when we remained moored to the bank it was our pleasure to study maps and charts of the waterways which lay ahead. Now we saw that other routes than the Intracoastal were open to us—bayous with names like Terrebonne, Boeuf, Chene and the famed Teche; the Atchafalaya River, Grand Lake and Plaquemine–Morgan City route; and there were unknown places to the west—such as Weeks Island and Cote Blanche—so strange to our ears that they seemed impossible to reach. Whenever it could be done without going too far out of the way, we planned to avoid the Intracoastal Canal. There was a touch of exploration and adventure in cruising the natural bayous, even though it made the distance somewhat longer. Thus we decided to go up Bayou Lafourche twelve miles to Lockport and follow from there a small canal to the southwest which crossed the Intracoastal and led to Bayou Terrebonne. This bayou could be followed to the Gulf, or in the other direction to Houma, a port on the Intracoastal Waterway.

This sort of planning was easy, and we looked forward with eagerness to resuming our voyage. There was another matter to be dealt with at this time, and even after a decision was reluctantly made, there was some doubt about our being able to carry it out. We had been in the South now for three years. Our house in Kentucky was in excellent hands, but it did need our attention. Also, it was two years since our last visit to Anna's mother at the end of the summer spent on the Cumberland River, and we were of course anxious to see her again. It seemed best to make this overland trip north in the summer, and we determined when under way again to look for some place where our shantyboat and the dogs could be left and cared for while we were away. Since we knew not a soul in this part of the country, the chances of finding a suitable place or person appeared to be slim.

Our hopes lay in Bayou Lafourche, but as we made our way toward Lockport they began to fade. We did not want to leave the dogs in town—they would surely get into trouble, and away from them we would imagine all manner of unhappy accidents.

Our first stop was at a bridge near a sugarhouse. This bridge was a pontoon bridge, like the three about Larose. It was a single barge across which a driveway ran from a sort of pier on one side to another opposite. To let a boat through, the barge was swung around sideways by cables and a gas engine, one end remaining fast to its pier. In this place, as it often happened, a mass of hyacinths had collected above the bridge, and our skiff was barely able to shove us through.

Finding no opening for us near the bridge we went on, but in a short distance tied up to the bank because of an approaching storm. It was a heavy one, with thunder, lightning, a downpour of rain, even some hail, and strong winds from different quarters. Before the storm broke I had managed to get the shutters to the windows closed—a feat which must be performed one-handed from the toe-hold along the outside of the cabin which we called the catwalk, holding on meanwhile by the other hand to the edge of the roof. Nevertheless I had to go out in the pouring rain to bail out the skiff, which was being filled. After the storm passed, the colors of sunset appeared low in the sky. A riding light was hung out, and we remained there until daybreak.

Farther up Lafourche, there appeared around a bend on the right a small shipyard. When nearer, we could read the sign on a gray building—Bollinger's Shipyard and Machine Shop. A small slip had been cut into the bank near the ways. Perhaps this was our place. We moored to the bank and I went up to the shop. The first Bollinger I met passed me on to Donald, who appeared to be head man. He was so cordial that my hopes rose. I stated our case. Donald walked with me down to the boat and we all talked in the cabin. When he left we had made a friend.

With such an agreeable person to deal with, arrangements for leaving the boat were soon completed. The shantyboat, skiff, and johnboat would be put in the slip, where they would be safe and out of the way. Donald would speak to Alcide Galiano, the farmer who lived across the road, about feeding the dogs. Thus the problem which yesterday had appeared so difficult, almost impossible, was solved with ease and dispatch. We could relax now, enjoy this new situation, and stay with the dogs until they felt at home.

The slip, which was just large enough to hold our boats, was right next to the marine ways, so we could see all that went on there—and hear, too, though Dick Bollinger said it was just as well that we couldn't understand the workmen's French. The boats that came in for repairs were mostly wooden-hulled Lafourche tugs and trawlers, and as they were often hauled out for painting or for small jobs on wheel, rudder, or planking, we had a succession of neighbors. When high on the ways they towered above our little shantyboat like a three-storied building.

To see the entire hull of a boat gives a new conception of its design. Only a small section is above the water line, and that is not as graceful and well-proportioned as the part which is underneath. Some of the crusty old tugs when pulled out of the water revealed an unsuspected beauty of line and form.

There were four Bollinger brothers, all of them young men, who ran the business and did most of the work, each having his particular branch, though all pitched in and did what was necessary when things were moving fast. They worked together well and enjoyed handling boats; with them it was more than just a business. In addition to the marine ways and machine shop, they owned three small tugs with which they did contract towing. All three might be in port for a few days, then one or all would vanish, the *Bud Bollinger* off to Lake Charles, perhaps, or the *Liberty* gone to tow some drilling equipment back among the stumps of interior Louisiana. The crew of each boat was made up of a captain and a boy or two, most of them from Larose, all eager as hounds to go out on a trip, the longer the better.

During our stay in the Bollinger shipyard we became better acquainted with the Lafourche countryside. In this middle section of the bayou, north of the Intracoastal, the land is in small holdings which are intensively cultivated, mostly in sugar cane, though we saw good corn and cattle. Each farm is a narrow strip between the bayou and the interior swamp, and since this depth is invariable, the size of each place is known by its frontage along the road, the distance being figured in arpents, which is like using the acre as a unit of linear measure. The narrowness of the farms puts the houses quite close together, and the Lafourche roads have the appearance of approaching a town that never materializes. Many of the places, especially the old ones, are shaded by live oaks, pecan, catalpa, or chinaberry trees, and the lush fields of cane, resembling thickly planted corn, crowd close to the neat farmyards. The cottages, also long and narrow, are likely to be designed after two or three basic patterns and painted in rather unusual colors. This gives the Lafourche countryside a charming aspect of harmonious variation which a planned community might fail to achieve.

The people of Lafourche, unlike the Baratarians, are landsmen, and generally their only use for a boat is to get to the other side of the bayou if a bridge is not handy. They are solidly French, even though a few of their names are German, Italian, Spanish and English. The Bollingers were of German descent. Donald was a husky blond, but his wife, dark and piquant, was entirely French, and Donald was, too, in many ways, probably having absorbed French traits in childhood. Galiano sounded to us like an Italian name, yet Alcide, of a reddish complexion, and the whole family were typical Louisiana French.

It had not taken us long to get acquainted with the Galianos, who were friendly and hospitable in the way country people are, whether in Louisiana or Kentucky. Yes, Alcide said, he would

feed the dogs during our absence. I made known our longing for fresh vegetables, and he supplied us abundantly with tomatoes, field peas, and corn, bringing it clear down to the boat. Mrs. Galiano was a charming person who showed us true kindness and understanding. There were two pretty daughters attending high school in Lockport, and two younger boys.

It was a pleasure to visit the Galianos—they were such a happy, lively, friendly family, and their immaculate house was so homelike. It was a true Lafourche cottage, painted apple green, its narrow end to the road. Once there was occasion to visit them after dark. When we climbed the bank and looked at the house, no lights could be seen. We went on, nevertheless, and at our knocking the door was opened on the customary brightness and activity inside. In bayou houses all the solid wooden shutters are closed at night to foil the mosquitoes. Nowadays the rooms are cooled and ventilated by electric ceiling fans, but how was such confinement tolerable in the old days? Perhaps the old-timers went to bed at dark in the summer, as we did.

It was two weeks after our arrival here before we were ready to leave on our journey to the north. All had been made shipshape, the skiff covered with a tarpaulin to keep out rain water. A large sack of dog food was left for Skipper and Sambo, who up to this point had not guessed what was going on.

It was hard to leave them, and we naturally had misgivings about them and our boat regardless of our complete confidence in the Bollingers and Galianos. But we were in for it now, and on July 12 we departed, anticipating our return with happier feelings than the trip ahead of us. Alcide took us in his car to Raceland, where we caught a bus to New Orleans, continuing from there on a train.

During the following days and weeks, in places which had the feel of home, with work to be done and friends to visit, the shantyboat and the dogs back in Louisiana ceased to be our prime concern. A letter from Donald Bollinger was reassuring—he said all was well, the dogs had adjusted themselves to the new conditions, and Sambo was well on the way to becoming a dog mechanic. There was one alarm while we were away, when a Gulf hurricane was reported and Bayou Lafourche lay in its path. Our boat would have some protection under the bank, but it was a relief to us when the storm changed its course.

Most of September had passed before a return to Louisiana was possible. On the way back, walking on the station platform at Mobile for a few minutes, the first breath of air from the Gulf—soft and sun-warmed, bearing the moisture and freshness of the sea, yet ever with portents of dread concealed in its gentleness—made us conscious of a world we had forgotten in our absence.

Alcide Galiano met us at Raceland, and Mrs. Galiano had supper ready for us when we reached their house. This was the beginning of a warm welcome from all our friends on Lafourche. Skipper and Sambo were rather indifferent about our return; especially Sambo, who continued to hang about the shop and to follow Alcide into the fields, sleeping under the Galiano house every night.

The boat was in good shape—a dry bilge and no invasion of ants, as Anna had feared. The cabin was dank and very dusty, a thick white layer on every level surface; but Anna soon made everything sweet and clean, while I took care of decks and boats and got all our gear in order.

After the wet and chilly weather in Michigan and Kentucky, it was good to be out in the warm sun again, to hear the singing mockingbirds, to go barefoot, and to see the expanse of blue sky.

Anxious as we were to get in motion again, more particularly to get into the open country, away from the dust and noise which seemed nearly to overwhelm us, we postponed our sailing to take advantage of this opportunity to pull the boat out on the

ways. The bottom of the hull had not been exposed since the launching nearly six years before. While we were sure that no major repairs were necessary, the seams must need some attention, and the hull below the water line could be given a coat of copper paint.

    We had to wait until a rush of work in the shipyard was over. One tug after another was hauled out on the ways, beginning with the *Gertrude,* fifty-six years old, which had sunk recently when her propeller pushed a log through the cypress planking. While the *Belfort* was out of the water, the refrigerator had to be cut off, so the captain gave us a quantity of fresh beef that would have spoiled. We tried to share with the Galianos, but instead they kept all of it for us in their refrigerator until we could use it. The meat was a welcome change from fish and crabs, though for a steady diet we would prefer fish and crabs to beef. We were getting to like crab gumbo with rice and okra as well as the natives of Louisiana do.

    All this pounding, sawing and shouting went on just outside our windows, and dust sifted down from the unpaved road, which because of an accident to a bridge now carried all the traffic, most of which normally followed the paved road on the other side. Then at evening the workmen left, the trucks ceased to run, and quiet enveloped the bayou. The silhouette of a weatherbeaten farmhouse and its surrounding oaks rose against the sunset sky. The shipyard was as if abandoned, and the boys on the idle tug fished for catfish, using bits of bread for bait. Often they strolled over to have a talk with us, and during our stay we got to know all of them, learning much of Cajun ways and thoughts. The one who visited us most often was Paul

Acheté, a relative of the friendly Estays in Larose. Paul had that love for the country and loyalty to his people which are Cajun traits. Even the boys who had been away, perhaps around the world with the army, were glad to get back to Louisiana, and they settled into their own ways with contentment; though as Paul said, "There is nothing here except water, grass and trees."

The Cajuns seemed to us like a big family, almost like a small nation with well-defined boundaries and a language of its own. Their French might vary from one district to another—Captain Falgoux of the *Liberty* gave us examples of words used on Bayou Teche which were different from those of Bayou Lafourche—but its use is universal, it is spoken by young and old. We saw few signs in French along the streets, other than an occasional *Bienvenue*, but some signs in English were almost French, like "Car wash and grease" or "Stop and eat, we fix you up." The scarcity of written or printed French is perhaps due to the fact that many of the older people never learned to read their language. The children nowadays are required to learn and use English in school, but many of them, having heard and spoken only French at home, find it hard going in the lower grades. Formerly, when they left school they were likely to forget the little English they did learn and revert to their mother tongue. The understanding and use of English is becoming much more widespread now that everyone has a chance to go to school.

During the time we were waiting our turn on the ways, the Galianos invited us one Sunday afternoon to go with them to Grand Island, which is on the Gulf shore near the mouth of Bayou Lafourche, if a bayou can be said to have a mouth. We were delighted to go, and were doubly grateful to our friends because we suspected that the trip had been arranged especially for us. One reason we were eager to see Grand Island was to find out why so many people liked to go there. It seemed that everyone on LaFourche was in the habit of visiting Grand Island, and all spoke of it with rapture.

The drive southward along Bayou Lafourche was in itself interesting enough to make the trip worth while. The land becomes lower, cane fields disappear, the bayou and boats take a more prominent place. Fishermen instead of farmers live in the cottages which have continued in an almost unbroken row down the bayou. Golden Meadow, the last town, is an active fishing port. Beyond it stretches a low marsh, the floating prairie, whose level expanse is broken only by sandy ridges where live oaks grow—the *chênières*. No signs of civilization can be seen except the built-up road and some oil wells, which make no distinction between water, swamp and solid land. Distant lakes and bays appear, and a long bridge is crossed, from which porpoises can be seen in the water and pelicans flying in even lines above it.

We had feared that Grand Island might be a sort of Coney Island, but not so. It is sand and sea wind and blue water, groves of trees on the leeward side and unobtrusive cottages where people enjoy themselves quietly. We drove to the eastern tip of the low, narrow island, which is seven and a half miles long, and looked across a channel at another island where stood a lighthouse and an ancient, brick-walled fort. A fishing boat passed through the channel, bound for Barataria Bay, the bayou, and perhaps the Mississippi River via the Harvey Canal. We thought of Jean and Paul Lafitte, whose pirate craft had often entered the bay through this pass. The buccaneers had been offered bribes by the British in 1814 to conduct the attackers to New Orleans through the back channels known so well to the smugglers; but though outlaws they were loyal to the United States and with their men fought bravely in the battle of New Orleans.

We found it delightful to walk on the sand, after the heavy soil and mud of the bayous inland—perhaps that is one reason the Lafourchais like Grand Isle. To the amusement of the Galiano boys, and all of us, the little crabs called *tourlourou* scuttled along the beach and popped into their holes before one could say— *tourlourou*. We waded in the warm salt water and looked out over the unruffled sea. Calm as it was then, the trees told us it was not always so. They were twisted and bent away from the south, and those on the windward side of the grove crouched close to the ground. We thought of hurricanes and Lost Island.

On the way back I talked with Alcide about the approaching cane harvest. The fields were now close-grown blocks of yellowing green. I was surprised to learn that the cane is cut by hand on Lafourche, not by machinery. The reason for this is the smallness of the farms and the fact that the sugarhouse can handle only limited quantities daily—Why, say the practical-minded Lafourche farmers, should we buy machinery to cut the cane faster than it can be processed? Alcide and his neighbors did not cut their own cane, however. This work was done by Negroes who came down from Mississippi every year. They were given neat houses to live in, respected and admired for their industry.

The stalks of cane are cut in such a way that they can be piled in long windrows, which are burnt to remove the dry blades, a task that used to be done by hand. Then the blackened stalks, looking like so much useless rubbish, are hauled in from the fields and loaded on trucks or railroad cars—a rickety, single-track line parallels the bayou. Along the railroad and by the roadsides, so numerous that they were a common feature in the Louisiana landscape, stood the derricks, consisting of a single pole and boom, used to hoist the harvested cane onto the cars and wagons. Near each derrick there was usually a queer structure like a sentry box on stilts. We were told that some person, often a woman, occupies this perch to read the scales at the end of the boom. The cane is weighed as it is loaded, and a strict record is made of each farmer's share before the load is hauled to the local sugarhouse. Here it is made into a coarse natural sugar and this is passed on to the big refineries, where the remainder of its value as food is removed.

A small section of new cane is planted each year in September, new-cut stalks being laid three together in a furrow, covered and left to sprout. A planting may be harvested four or five successive years. The growing of sugar cane requires hot weather and abundant rain; on both counts Louisiana is an excellent place for it.

I asked so many questions about all this that it was suggested that I stay and work in the harvest. Much of the casual information I picked up came from Mr. Melançon, who lived in the next house down the road. He visited us frequently because he had time on his hands, having been injured not long ago by a dragline which was ditching one of his fields. He was a queer fellow, tall and gaunt, abrupt and unpredictable as a boat-tailed grackle. The growing of sugar cane was his passion, and he liked to talk about it, though his English was about as crippled as his walking. His second interest, which rounded out the year and kept him as busy as he liked to be, was trapping.

Lulu Melançon, another capable Cajun youngster, came to see us also. One day he said he was going back in the woods. It seemed something like an invitation, so I said I would go along.

We rode a tractor to the end of the farmland, and then Lulu led the way afoot into the swampy woods until we came to a ditch and pirogue, a beautiful old one made of a single cypress log. It was so flat and short that I had some doubts about its holding both of us, but Lulu said it would. We launched it in the narrow ditch, and Lulu paddled, sitting behind me—my first pirogue ride. We entered a wider stream crossing at right angles. I was disappointed that we saw no alligators, but we did come to a banana grove, the trees hanging with unripe fruit. I think this was what Lulu wanted to show me because I had been so curious about the banana trees in their yard.

Mr. Melançon took an unexpected interest in my painting and asked me to make a picture of his accident. That it might be authentic, he led me to the field where the dragline had been working, showed me the stump against which he had been nearly crushed when the machine had turned farther around than it was in the habit of doing; then he took me a few miles down the road to the present location of the very dragline. I did not know what all this was about, but made the picture, a small oil painting of the field and woods, the yellow dragline, Melançon in blue denims, and, if you looked carefully, the snake which had precipitated the incident.

Perhaps no one saw the snake in so small a painting, but the boys at the shipyard liked the picture and recognized Melançon at once. When I showed it to him, he took a long look and said, "I guess I'll go over and see how my wife is getting along with the ironing." Lulu came aboard later and asked how much I wanted for the picture. I told him to take it along. Before we left, Melançon sent us a basket of sweet potatoes, not very good ones but the best he had, no doubt. He and Lulu had been kind to us in many ways. Some time later word reached us that the picture of Melançon's accident had been used by his lawyer in a suit for damages.

When our shantyboat was hauled out on the ways, the hull was found to be sound, needing only some caulking and paint. The copper paint was sprayed on by one of the shipyard men, relieving me of a disagreeable task. Machines have their uses.

We continued to live on the boat while it was perched up in the air, on a level with the rest of the world and with dry land all around us. It had a solidity to which we were not accustomed—

there is a give to it in water when you walk across the cabin, and even small waves rock it a little. It was strange to see a tug pass and have the boat remain steady as a house.

On Tuesday, October 10, we were slid back into the water and we got under way soon after the launching. Skipper and Sambo came dashing aboard at the first sound of the engine. We had thought that Sambo might prefer to remain with Alcide, but now there was no doubt as to whom he would follow. We waved good-bye to the Bollinger Shipyard and Machine Shop, which we had first sighted nearly three and a half months before.

The run to Lockport was short. On the way we saw a reminder of the days when Bayou Lafourche was a part of the Mississippi River system—the wreck of a steamboat along the shore. It was a small hull, mostly under water, but its shape, towing knees, upper deck with two holes for stacks, hog-chain braces, rudder posts, and the remains of a stern wheel—all this identified it as an old-style towboat. Who will tell the story of bayou steamboating?

The first Lockport buildings we came to were also relics of steamboat days. We passed on, slipped under the bridge with two feet to spare and turned left into the small canal at which the town ended abruptly. A pontoon bridge lay ahead. This was opened at our signal and we went on just far enough to be in open country. We pulled into a small slip on the north bank, moored the boat, and cleaned off the roadside dust for good.

VI

This harbor held no particular attraction for us, nor did we have any reason for remaining near Lockport; but it was so good to be to ourselves in the open country, away from roads, dust, and noise, that we were content to linger here until the spirit should move us to travel on.

The low shores of the canal allowed us to overlook from our deck the level country which surrounded us, a privilege that had been lacking when we were under the higher banks of Bayou Lafourche. Here was a wide plain of grass and scattered trees extending to the remote forest wall, the green surface broken by streaks and patches of water which reflected the sky.

One quarter of the landscape was taken up by the town of Lockport, whose small houses merged into a varicolored pattern of squares and triangles spaced with the loose, rounded forms of trees. None of the houses crossed the canal to our side, but a few straggled along the shore until almost opposite our landing.

From our outpost in the prairie we watched the little town in a detached way, much as if looking through a telescope. Its people and their ways became familiar, not as neighbors and acquaintances we might go and talk with, but rather as characters in a play. Little was to be seen in the Lockport streets and yards during these hot September days, but evidences of an inward life drifted across the water. In midmorning there came a smell of cottonseed oil heating on the stoves and of onions cooking, unvarying preliminaries to Cajun dinners; and during the noon hour, if the breeze were right, snatches of a radio news broadcast in orthodox French. In the early afternoon Lockport seemed to enjoy a siesta, from which it wakened as the shadows grew longer. The place was lively in the cool evenings, when the ladies visited and children played in the open, and voices of men and boys were heard along the shore as pirogues were taken from their low sheds and launched in the canal. Dogs barked and were answered by Skipper and Sambo. Sambo would swim over to Lockport after dark, to return dripping in the early morning.

One day, probably the opening of hunting season, men and boys embarked in pirogues with dogs and guns, and set off down the canal toward the woods. We marveled at the heavy load a slight pirogue could carry; one was never seen to sink or turn over.

We rowed to Lockport now and then to go to stores or post office—there are always many errands when a town is near. Since most of the Bollingers lived in Lockport we kept in touch with them, and we were in Donald's house the evening news came that one of their tugboats, the *Agnes Reilly*, had run onto a snag in a part of Louisiana to the north where we had not supposed there was any navigable water. The Bollingers were not alarmed by the mishap, and the *Reilly* got off without their assistance.

One Sunday we wandered through a carnival which was in progress in the main street of Lockport. There were two rows of stands, with some sort of noisemaker in each one. Above the tumult a loud voice could be heard announcing bingo numbers in both French and English. We did not see the dancing; it would not be until evening. This is a favorite amusement on Lafourche. Young and old take part with gusto, and every town has a large dance hall.

Movies seem to be popular, too. Some Lockport youngsters who had paddled over to see the strange campboat were well up on the latest pictures and also television programs. One of the boys named Aubrey—he preferred to be called Bloody Ranger—told us he saw all the shows, which meant three a week.

These boys were curious about us, where we came from, how we lived and what we were doing. They answered questions as freely as they asked them. Like their parents they wasted no words and spoke with the sharpness and lack of grace common to many Cajuns. We liked to have the boys around. They took a keen interest in some books, *Kon-Tiki* for one, which Anna showed them. One day they watched me assembling the binoculars which had been mailed to us in parts. Anna was helping by reading the directions aloud. "Can't your husband read?" asked Bloody Ranger, without surprise. Perhaps his father, like many of the older French people, could not. There will be no illiteracy in the latest generation, and in the towns, at least, a waning use of Cajun French.

We wished that Bloody Ranger was with us the day two cowboys galloped up to the boat; or perhaps these everyday cowboys would not arouse the admiration of boys whose standards were formed by television. They were real cowboys, nevertheless, and their business with us was to ask us to move our shantyboat out of the slip for half an hour that they might bring in a bargeload of cattle to unload there. In Louisiana even cowpunching has some boating in it.

For the most part our days were quiet and unbroken, giving long-submerged thoughts and projects a chance to rise to the surface. We tuned our instruments and played often, did some extra reading. I took up my writing again and had some good days painting, occasionally leaving the boat to make sketches about Lockport. Once, when making a quick drawing of the Lafourche bridge, I was sharply questioned by the town constable, but this time I was not taken for a spy; it seems that all picture-makers were suspect in Lockport because some traveling photographers had once fleeced the public.

After a long day spent within the cabin or on the shady deck, we liked to go out on the water in the evening to see the afterglow and its reflections. The Louisiana sunsets are brilliant displays—such a vast sky over the flat land, and cloud formations of endless variety. One evening when we had rowed down the canal a ways we discovered a vegetable garden tended by a Lockport man who paddled out to it in a pirogue after his day's work in town was done. Though this was October, he was hopefully planting beans, had a new crop of pole beans already in bloom, potatoes coming up and cabbage plants set out. In southern Louisiana the best gardening is done in spring and fall, the summers being too hot for most crops except okra and field peas. The scarcity of green vegetables was a trial for us. Not much could be bought in the stores, and our home-canned supply, even the Greenville pickled beets, was all gone. Pokeweed was still our best source of greens; though the red, blooming stalks were eight feet high, I could find tender shoots at the tip and branching.

This gardener helped us out by giving us some small, pale-colored squash which he called "melitons," as near as we could understand the name. The vine had climbed a tree where the pear-shaped melitons hung like fruit. Like all gardeners, the man had his troubles. Blackbirds were causing havoc in general and field mice were eating his peanuts. The most serious difficulty, however, was lack of rain.

The drought had put us on short rations of drinking water, which in Louisiana comes from rain-filled cisterns. These are wooden tanks above the ground, circular, made of cypress staves, tapering slightly toward the top, which is often capped with a roof like a flattened cone. The cisterns stand on short legs at the corner, often at two corners, of every house, at once an ornament and a necessity. Their capacity varies according to the size of the house, but I think they are generally smaller than Kentucky dug cisterns, for here the rainfall is more frequent and abundant. The Lockport cisterns were almost empty now, and we hesitated to accept water even from Mrs. Bollinger, who was generously insistent. Fortunately the new Lockport city water system was nearing completion. It was a great day for the citizens and for us when a truck with blaring loud-speakers cruised the streets alternating jazz music with the often-repeated proclamation, which we could hear from our side of the canal, that the new city water was "ready for human consumption."

The long-awaited rains now began. An autumn storm drenched the country, filling all the cisterns whether the water was wanted or not. After the last of the dust had been washed from our roof, we collected as much drinking water as could be stored in reserve jugs and jars.

These rains sprouted the newly planted cane and raised the hopes of the gardeners. They also stirred up in us a desire to be on our way, to leave the town completely and to see what was ahead on the canal. That evening we took a last look at the dull-red board cottage under the live oaks across the canal, every detail of which had become so well known, and next morning some of the Lockport people must have noticed the little campboat was missing.

The course we had laid out to the west, with Houma as our next port, was in a zigzag direction, like that of a sailboat beating into the wind. The narrow canal on which we left Lockport had formerly been a link of the Intracoastal Waterway, connecting Bayou Lafourche to Bayou Terrebonne, but now that a more direct route has been dug, the old way is seldom used. Only one boat passed while we lay along its shore—the tug *Jupiter*, towing two covered barges, presumably of raw sugar on the way to the refinery. Because of its disuse this canal contained many hyacinths. They were a hindrance from beginning to end, and in order to see our way among the floating islands, I often rode on the roof as a lookout, calling directions to Anna, who was steering in the skiff. It made an unforgettable picture to look down on the trim skiff and the wake it made in the still water; and on Anna sitting erect with one hand on the steering lever, though from my elevation only her lovely chin and throat were visible under the pink flowered sunbonnet—the sunbonnet I had seen in a row with others all different in a store window as I was sauntering through the Ohio River town of Pomeroy, long before I knew Anna; the store rather dingy otherwise, kept by the old man who had made the sunbonnets. Attracted by their prettiness, as of old-fashioned flowers, I had bought this one on a sudden impulse, thinking I might find someone who would like to wear it.

From the roof one had as well a wide view over the land. The different kinds of plants and grasses were not mingled but grew in definite areas, due no doubt to certain variations of soil condition or elevation. Thus the wild landscape had the appearance of farmland with marked fields differing in color, texture and height of growth; not planted in the crops we know but with new ones, as if it were a strange world.

Always the golden land was broken by water of the deepest blue where white birds waded.

At times the lilies became so thick that they blocked our passage, and while waiting for wind or current to break up the jam, we explored the new territory. At one point a narrow channel led to a round lake where we saw a campboat, the wreck of another, and some half-hearted crab fishermen tracing their lines.

Where the land was firm we threaded our way through the woods or strolled in open pasture land. On one of these walks Skipper was again bitten by a snake, a cottonmouth moccasin only two feet long but thick as a man's wrist. The poor dog became sick at once, her head and neck swelled until she looked like a caricature of herself; yet in a few days she was perfectly well and able to continue her aggressive warfare against all snakes.

Sometimes the marsh gave way to a solid shore two or three feet above the water. One of these "islands"—called Eagle Island on our map, which indicated a short road there by a dotted line—was large enough for cattle raising. It had the appearance of a western ranch, with weathered buildings among the oaks, rambling sheds, haystacks and corrals; the dock and skiff being purely Louisiana, however. Here the people lived who had roused our wonder when they had passed us near Lockport, their skiff loaded with groceries on the return trip, the ladies with umbrellas for parasols.

If it were possible anywhere, one could live in peace on Eagle Island. As we sailed by, it seemed to be a world in itself, isolated in space, having its own sun and air; the very buildings lost in meditation, and nary a person to be seen about them.

Now the shores became swampy and bordered with reeds. Close to the canal on one side was a long lake; on the other, a forest. Out of this suddenly appeared a huge tugboat with a string of barges which passed in front of us like a freight train. We had reached the Intracoastal Waterway.

Looking up and down to see if there were any more like that, we crossed the big canal and continued southward. Our small canal became even more narrow, a straight ditch between high banks. The masses of hyacinths, which had been with us all the way, now became so thick that it was impossible to force a way through them. When we shut off the motor we noticed that they were slowly drifting in the direction we were headed, toward the Gulf. The oncoming myriads behind us made escape back to the Intracoastal impossible. We were trapped by the weight and power of the soft flowers. Drifting along at their slow pace we looked at the map again. Bayou Terrebonne was less than a mile ahead, and a bridge crossed the canal just before the junction. What if it were a pontoon bridge and all these weeds were packing in a tight mass against it? I climbed to the roof and with our new binoculars could make out that it was a lift bridge, that it spanned the canal, and that the lilies were passing under it.

After an hour's drifting we were near enough to signal. The bridge tender appeared from somewhere and began to turn a crank. One end of the bridge raised—it looked like the drawbridge of an old castle. The man stopped cranking and shouted, "Is that high enough?" I thought our chimneys would clear at the side where the bridge was higher. Keeping the boats lined up and away from the fenders with our poles, we drifted through the narrow opening at a faster rate. Immediately past the bridge we entered Bayou Terrebonne, which was at a right angle to the canal. The stream of lilies turned left, seaward. We started the engine, turned to the right, pushed through a few rods of weeds, and entered open water.

Terrebonne, narrow and crooked, overhung with trees and Spanish moss, was a true bayou, quite different from Lafourche with its river traits. It wound through an out-of-the-way country where the past lingered in gray gables of old houses which peered out from among the trees, in the quaint wooden bridges which were opened and closed by hand. One of these had no mechanism whatever. It pivoted in the center and was opened by a sturdy fellow who set his back against it and, walking backward on a curved boardwalk under the bridge, pushed it around so that we could pass by. Several campboats lay along the shore, and from one of them a man paddled along with us in a pirogue for a ways, showing us several nice mullet he had caught in a cast net.

We stopped at one point to pick a few meager bunches of bananas from trees growing close to the water; not the store kind, but good to eat when at last they ripened. Now we felt we were shantyboating in a tropic land, and we looked for alligators more hopefully. After the bananas it was not so much of a surprise to discover a grove of oranges as we walked along a road during the midday stop. We picked a few which hung over the fence. They were small, like tangerines, and called satsumas, as we learned when we saw them later in a local store. These and a similar fruit called mandarins are the oranges of Louisiana.

We pulled up short of the city of Houma, but the rural bay-

ou had already changed to a narrow harbor with many trawlers and oyster boats. One of these, the *Irresistible*, docked just above us to unload sacked oysters into a truck. Crowding the banks were picturesque sheds and buildings, some the homes of Negroes with open back doors and yards running down to the water.

Houma, though fifty miles from the Gulf, to which it is connected only by narrow, winding bayous, is a busy fishing port, having docks and shipyards, sea-food packers, net makers, and dealers in fishermen's supplies; all crowded along the narrow stream which must serve as harbor.

Next morning we moved farther up Bayou Terrebonne, crossed the Intracoastal Waterway, and found a mooring among the docks, bridges, and buildings of the city, which nearly swallowed up the narrow stream. After trying our shantyboat to a row of piling, we climbed the steep bank and found ourselves on the main street. An ice cream stand nearby had an outside tap which was a convenient source of drinking water.

Houma, which is pronounced "home-a," was the largest place we had been in since leaving New Orleans. It gave us a chance to do some city shopping, though our most important purchase was a cast net which could have been bought at many of the waterside country stores in Louisiana. I had wanted a cast net ever since I saw the first one. After some looking about and comparing of prices which did not vary, we bought one at Pitre's, a fisherman's store located on Main Street, according to the address, but more properly on Bayou Terrebonne near the Intracoastal. Nine feet in diameter, the net was considered four and a half feet long, since that was its length when held by the center. At $2.50 per foot, our net cost $11.25—a high figure it seemed at first; but when we considered how many hours it would take to weave a foot of net, and how each succeeding foot increased in area with the spread of the net, the price asked was reasonable. We never regretted buying it; our cast net soon paid for itself in bait and fish caught. Though I never became very expert, I had much pleasure from casting, and some excitement. It is such a direct and simple way of fishing. The net was decorative when spread over the end of the cabin to dry; and it brought us close to the Cajuns.

After one night in Houma we were glad to escape from the city noises and smells, from the unclean water. It seemed best to follow the Intracoastal westward, though we were tempted to go into Bayou Black; or to follow an outbound fishing boat through a small bayou called Le Carpe, another of those leading from Houma to the Gulf. We wanted very much to reach the gulf shore, but our maps informed us that there would be shorter routes farther west; in fact, the Intracoastal canal seemed to skirt the shore in some places.

For a few miles out of Houma the canal wound through a higher land which might almost be called rolling; or perhaps the "hills" were merely heaps of spoil from dredging.

The breeze this day was so light that it would have been unnoticed on land, but coming directly against us it cut our speed to almost nothing. Although this made no difference to the engine, which just kept spinning away regardless of whether the boat was moving or not, it was something of a strain on us; so in midafternoon we nosed into a small opening called Bonvillain Canal, a wooded place with willows and even a few cottonwoods growing near the water; and on slightly higher ground farther back were oak, ash, hackberry and blackthorn. I took advantage of this source of hardwood to replenish our stock of cook wood, of which a large reserve must be carried in this wet, grassy country. While I was chopping, a big towboat came by—one of the Hoaglands from Paducah—and evidently not seeing us among the trees, passed at full speed. Its waves banged our shantyboat repeatedly against a heavy branch with such force that Anna, alone on board, expected disaster; but luckily only the edge of the deck roof was bashed in. We then pulled the boat farther into the canal, got a gangplank out to shore, and tied up for the night. I spent the rest of the afternoon repairing the deck and finishing the woodcutting.

We now entered a series of long straight reaches where the canal and the marsh seemed to go on without end. No turning could be seen, no break in the level horizon. Though the skiff churned away, we seemed to be standing still in the midst of infinite space. The unvarying shores flowed slowly past us. Out of the nothingness far ahead, a spot would appear on the bank which might materialize into a bush or stunted tree, an empty trapper's cabin or a signboard. Here comes one which looks like a sign. Is it the next Intracoastal Waterway five-mile post? No, it is something different, and we become curious about it. At length we can see that it is a rough board with the Cajun inscription "No Hunning Allow" in crude letters. It passes as if moving under its own power and slowly recedes astern until lost in the shimmering distance.

One afternoon as we cruised along I happened to discover that the bottom of the shantyboat was fouled with hyacinths, not attached in any way but held there by the upward pressure of the buoyant float on each plant. I tried to pry them off with an oar and to drag them off with a piece of rope, but these methods were ineffectual. Then, without stopping the engine—Anna steering the while, as she often did when the housework was done—I worked one of the gangplanks ahead of the boat and by means of lines on each end, dragged the plank underneath the boat from bow to stern. This cleared the hull of the tangled lilies, which floated astern in an amazing quantity. The boat's speed increased immediately—or so I imagined; it must have made a difference.

Even at our best speed, with no long stops and no hindrance from wind, a full day's run would be no more than twelve or fourteen miles—an intolerably slow pace to the modern traveler, but fast enough for us. It did not shrink the extent of the marsh, as speed would have done. We enjoyed the vastness of the terrain to its full. For whole days no person was to be seen, except for the crews of passing boats, and the boats, like floating bits of wreckage on the ocean, were the only visible reminders of the inhabited world. Even the tugs seemed to be farther apart in this immensity of space; yet we still had to be cautious, and if possible steered into a small bayou or side channel when we wished to stop.

At one of these chance landings we were surprised to see a motorboat approach bearing a man and three children. After he had satisfied himself about the strange campboat which had landed in his territory, the man chatted for some time, while the children stared and giggled. His conversation was mostly about the prospects of the trapping season which would soon open, though we tried to get him to speak of his family's life in the marsh and the children's schooling. The man's name was Duet, and he was one of a family of twenty children—eleven boys and nine girls. He said his mother was still living. Besides this personal information he told us about the pirogue trails which allowed the trappers to paddle about in a marsh impassable to a man on foot. These long ditches, only a yard wide, are dug through the spongy soil by a heavy motorboat which has a rotating blade on its bow, a strange-looking craft we had already seen and wondered at.

At length we reached Bayou Cocodrie, so wide in one place that it had the appearance of a long lake. We felt like real pilots as we steered along the line of red buoys which marked the channel. In the quiet morning it was like navigating among the clouds, for the smooth water reflected the sky almost perfectly, and the distant shores were but thin strips of green.

A thin faint line appeared across our course, gradually darkening as we approached it, and taking on the green hue of trees. Then the bayou narrowed and became a winding track through a dense forest. Now at the turn of the season the thick, soft foliage of the cypress trees was a golden green through which the straight gray trunks gleamed in the sun. On higher ground within the forest were many other kinds of trees—gum, maple, oak, ash, and some we did not know—all of them beginning to show the red and yellow of autumn. It was a sight we had not expected to see in Louisiana. Although the brilliance of color rivaled that of Michigan in the fall, pendants of Spanish moss and sprays of palmetto reminded us that this was the South.

Farther into the depths of the forest, Bayou Cocodrie joined Bayou Black. Here we turned aside from the Intracoastal to tie up our fleet and eat a late dinner. Across the bayou, at a cabin in a clearing, a man was roughing out a pair of oars with an ax from cypress logs just cut. When I rowed across to talk with him he warned me that we lay in a dangerous place because the tug *Slade Brown* frequently went up Bayou Black and her barges scraped the bank in making the turn. We had thought to lay over there for a night, but now this plan was abandoned and we made ready to cast off. Just as we were leaving, a small, half-cabin motorboat with a tarpaulin over the open cockpit, which had gone up Bayou Black earlier, returned with a load of children. The boat stopped at the dock near the cabin, put ashore three youngsters with books under their arms, and proceeded westward with the others.

It was sunset as we sailed through the darkening woods, our goal the junction of Bayou Black and Bayou Chene, where the Intracoastal made a short cut-off. This we reached in good time since it was only a mile and a half away. We bent to the left, then to the right a few hundred yards farther on, rounding a sharp point into Bayou Chene. Opposite the point, on the left bank of Bayou Black, were a few small houses, the most prominent being a tiny store with a dock and a signboard which read "Curtis Verret."

We landed now on the Bayou Chene side of the triangular island which is bounded by Chene, Black, and the Intracoastal cut-off, each side being about a quarter of a mile long.

The forest we had entered that day cast a spell over us which was stronger than the urge to go on to new places. We could have ended our voyage and stayed there for good, certain that nothing finer than this could be seen in Louisiana; yet after a while the spell would be broken and we would sail westward to find a land entirely different, one for which our imagination would prepare us no better than it had done for the forests of Chene.

Like our voyage, the passage of time and the change of the season seemed to have come to a stand. Who was it that, like us, had stayed his course to watch the ripening forest, where the cypress became an arrowhead of ruddy gold, where the maple, gum and oak blazed among the restrained colors of ash and hackberry; where the dark, glossy green of the live oak was a symbol of life everlasting?

On those fair November days, past the heat of summer but still delightfully warm, we lived to a large extent in the open; had our meals on deck and often lingered there in the afternoon to read and work; or roamed abroad on our little island or farther into the woods, threading a way among the palmettos, watching the birds and ever keeping an eye open for snakes. I continued to fish and cast, even though the catch was meager. A clam bed which I discovered in a cove was a more dependable source of food, and I picked up many bucketfuls from the muddy bottom which I could just reach when lying on the deck of the johnboat.

In our exploration of the adjacent waterways, we made a long run in the skiff down Bayou Chene; though not far enough to reach Bayou Penchant by which we could have passed into Bayou Shaffer and thence into Sweetbay Lake, a widening of the Atchafalaya River. The bayou was an open way through the woods which seemed to crowd into the stream; for often the massive, tapering trunk of a cypress stood in the shallow water, surrounded by a miniature forest of grotesque "knees," whose rounded tops looked as if they had been polished and gilded.

There were small islands on the sharp bends, and a few farmhouses in old clearings on the higher shores of the bayou, unkempt places where the wilderness was never quite subdued.

The dock, boats and gear at each place indicated that the operations of the inhabitants were not confined to their fields and woods, while the life on the campboats we passed was more frankly that of the hunter, fisherman and trapper; but these people often had a little clearing on shore, a shed, perhaps even a cow. There was really not much difference between living on water and on land; it was merely a shift of emphasis.

We had our boat tied up with the main deck toward the shore, where we soon made a tiny clearing of our own. The boat was kept from swinging in the wind or current—one as variable as the other—by a pole or two driven into the mud at the outer end. This was a favorite position because it gave a clear view up and down the stream from our large side windows. The view down the bayou at this point—we always felt that the direction in which the Gulf lay was downstream—was a constant joy. At the end of a short reach, directly in the line of the stream, which there swung to the right, lay the diminutive Bayou Black Settlement, as the map called it; not so far away but that we could hear the voices of children and the singing of the mockingbird which the clearing was large enough to attract. The handful of houses was close to the water, before a continuous wall of trees. The little store faced us directly. Often at its dock a trawler would be moored, a passer-by on her way to or from the fishing grounds to the south, and gone the next time we looked. The only other building we could see plainly was the small church, painted green with a red roof and white cross. The Verrets' house was partly visible and one other; that was about all of Bayou Black Settlement, or as we came to call it, Bayou Chene.

Close to us, on the island shore beyond some cypresses, a small campboat lay in a slip. An old man lived there with a companion named Pete, a dark, silent, barefoot young man whom we rarely saw and never heard speak.

The old man—named Frank Verret, a relative of the Verrets at the store—came to see us the first morning. He was a friendly soul, shy and gentle; and lonely, perhaps, since he visited us so often. His kindness embarrassed us sometimes, for he made an effort to get us anything we might have expressed a liking for, and gave us things we thought he could better have used himself.

Mr. Verret's greatest service lay in telling us much lore of the

bayous and information about the Settlement. We learned that the inhabitants depended entirely on the bayous for transportation and communication, the nearest road being four miles away. The storekeeper got in his supplies by boat—the same motorboat we had seen bringing home the school children, for Curtis Verret operated a school bus along Bayous Chene and Black, picking up the children at the scattered houses and boats, and taking them to a point where a road and school bus were accessible. Mail was carried along Bayou Chene by boat—this was Marine Route No. 2, Morgan City, Louisiana. The aquatic counterpart of the rural carrier made two trips a week. Mass was held in the church one Sunday a month, the storekeeper's boat meeting the priest at the road's end in the morning of that day and ferrying him back after the service.

We had gone to Verret's store soon after our arrival on Bayou Chene. It was fun to land at the dock among other small boats and go along the boardwalk to the porch of the one-room building, where one of the Verrets, coming out of their house nearby, would welcome us and proceed to open the store; the whole affair being more of a social call than business.

Inside we were reminded of a store in the Kentucky mountains. The space for stock was so small that nothing was kept unless the trade really demanded it; yet more varied items would be pulled out of corners, from drawers and under something else, than would ever be expected in so small a place. We made out very well except in the matter of dog food, and Mr. Verret obligingly brought a few cans of this out from town so that Sambo and Skipper might have an occasional change from their diet of clams and wild food.

Mr. and Mrs. Verret were amiable, intelligent people with a large and worthy family, all with that energy and quickness common to the Louisiana French. When the oldest boy went by, his vigorous strokes sent the skiff through the water with a bow wave and a wake behind, though his errand might be just to our boat to bring us a squirrel or rabbit. The Verrets were kind to us and we felt close to them, as if the fewness of the people and the isolation of the place made such contacts more to be treasured. All the family came to visit with us, even Grandfather Verret, a hale old man from Lake Palourde, or Clam Lake. After the opening of the trapping season—that great day of days in Louisiana, when all the men and boys take to the woods, and pelts of muskrat and mink stretched on boards begin to appear on inner walls—these thoughtful people supplied us with fresh game—coon, squirrel, rabbit, muskrat, and once a large owl ready dressed, with instructions to boil it for a long time. It was tough, even so.

The bayou people eat many of the marsh birds, the ibis for one, which Mrs. Verret called, as nearly as we could make out, "bec-cross." Strangely enough, the Verrets had a flock of tame ducks. We mistook them for wild birds when we first saw them swimming along the bayou shore, quite some distance from their home.

We went to Morgan City with the Verrets one day, beginning the trip with a ride of four or five miles in their motorboat to the road where their small truck was parked; then along a shell road which followed the bayou beneath mossy oaks and pecans, past cabins and scattered plantation houses, all silvery from years of exposure to sun and rain. The last part of the ride was over a highway, but even that had a Louisiana character.

Morgan City was a small bustling place which had the appearance of a seaport, a New Orleans in miniature, with docks and boats along the wide Atchafalaya River.

Returning, we wondered how the launch could hold this truckload of stuff and four people. The most bulky item was soft drinks in cases. There were sacks of feed for the bayou cows and chickens, sacks of beans, rice, potatoes, onions and flour; a box of fresh bread, a bundle of brooms, ice, two boxes of fresh milk and some cases of canned goods. Arriving at the dock they stowed as much of this as possible into the motorboat and piled the rest into a skiff which was towed behind. It was well that the water was smooth. When the store was reached, the children came out and all was unloaded and carried into the store with great haste, as if a storm threatened. This was the way of the Verrets.

We found that Sunday was the busiest day on Bayou Chene. Fishing boats and joeboats were out to make Sunday visits. The store was open, and customers, some of them Negroes, paddled by, returning with their pirogues loaded with groceries and soft drinks.

Pirogues were not so common in these parts. Skiffs were more widely used, and these were rowed in a manner novel to us. The oarlocks were on the ends of upright boards which extended perhaps two feet above the gunwales and continued the flare of the boat's sides. The oarsmen stood up, faced the bow and pushed on a pair of long, heavy oars, something in the manner of a man walking on crutches. The practice was so universal here and to the westward that we began to look upon our own way of rowing—sitting down, facing the stern and pulling on the oars—as rather awkward and unnatural, though we never changed our johnboat into a pushing skiff.

Only one commercial tow passed here—a small fleet of equipment for oil well drilling or prospecting. A trawler went by now and then, but only one of these stopped at our boat. It happened on the day that I was making the final test and adjustment of our new binoculars, a process which called for a sheet of paper with crossed lines on it, placed fifty feet away. Since there was no room in the cabin or on shore, I had set up a post in the water and fastened the target to that. While I was looking at it, a trawler passed going north, then another coming south. I turned

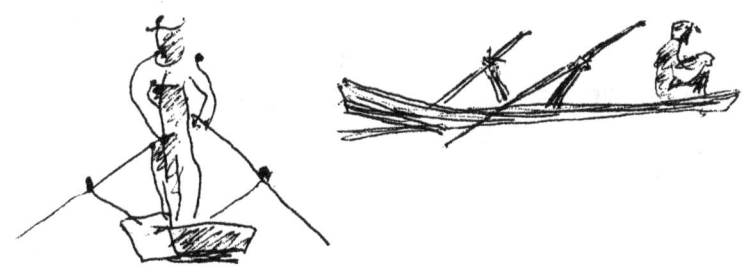

the glasses toward these boats, but so briefly that I did not realize it was the same boat going and returning, operated by the same man. After I had viewed him the second time he turned his boat around, stopped close to us and shouted something in an angry tone. I rowed out to see what was the matter. It seemed that I was a suspicious character, a spy no doubt, and he was going to do something about it. I explained how I was testing the binoculars and pointed out the card I had been sighting. After some talk he calmed down and went on his way. Another day he stopped again, all smiles and friendliness, and asked if he could bring us anything from town.

Toward the latter part of November the weather changed. We were glad of rain, for drinking water was again scarce. This was followed by north winds and an air so keen that we burned a fire in the fireplace all day for warmth. After a while the weather moderated, the days became warm and sunny; but it was winter now, even in Louisiana. Interest in our voyage was revived and at length we cast off, happy as always to be on the move again. Two miles along Bayou Chene brought us to Bayou Boeuf, which they pronounce "Beff." Following the Intracoastal route we now turned left. The wider stream led us past more gray houses among the green oaks and deciduous trees, whose autumn colors seemed even more brilliant since the frost. As Morgan City was neared, the shores became industrial. We saw docks, floating equipment, sawmills, and at last the trains whose whistles had sometimes reached us in the forest.

Just a mile short of the Atchafalaya River we passed a small cable ferry which crossed the Intracoastal, and then we turned south, leaving Bayou Boeuf to enter Bayou Shaffer. In a short distance we tied up to a fairly open shore on the left, along which ran a dirt road to the ferry. This was our Morgan City harbor. Our roundabout course from the Mississippi River was somewhat farther than the ninety-five miles along the Intracoastal. We had left Harvey seven months before.

VII

Nearly a year previous to our arrival at Morgan City, when we were drifting down the Mississippi River, with Louisiana on both shores, we came to a wide opening on the western side which the map called Lower Old River but which a local fisherman had spoken of as the Mud Ditch. We might have thought that this was a tributary stream except for the curious fact that a considerable volume of water was pouring into it from the Mississippi. This water finds an outlet to the Gulf of Mexico through the Atchafalaya River, which begins at the Mud Ditch and flows in a southerly direction for 140 miles; a short cut to the Gulf compared with the 302-mile distance on the Mississippi from this point to its mouth.

In order to keep to our original plan and continue down the Mississippi to New Orleans, it was necessary to row our shantyboat across this outflowing current, a feat we were able to accomplish by good luck and hard pulling on sweeps and oars. Had our attempt failed we would have been carried through the Mud Ditch and down the Atchafalaya, it being an inexorable law of drifting shantyboats that they go downstream only, and never retrace their course against the current for even a short distance.

If the river currents had decided that we drift down the Atchafalaya instead of the Mississippi, we would have missed seeing Baton Rouge and New Orleans and that section of the river which is navigable for ocean ships. A voyage down the

Atchafalaya, however, would have had its own rewards. It would have been more adventurous, for the Atchafalaya is a wild river, according to maps and to tales of river people. It flows through a wild country and about halfway in its course becomes nearly lost in an indefinite network of swampy bayous. Then comes a series of lakes, shallow but sizable bodies of water. We would have had to wait for a favorable breeze to sail down Grand Lake, nearly twenty miles long. Just south of the lake is Morgan City, twenty miles above the mouth of the river and the only town on its banks.

As it was, we reached Morgan City by way of New Orleans and the Intracoastal Waterway, with detours. On studying a map of the region, the land and water areas appeared to be about equal in size. Lakes, bays and connecting bayous form a network of water which cuts the land into islands of varying shapes and sizes, much as if it were a jigsaw puzzle with some of the pieces joined together, the cracks between them representing the bayous, and the missing pieces the lakes.

Morgan City, on Tiger Island, looks westward over a wide expanse of the Atchafalaya River called Berwick Bay. The southern boundary of the town is Bayou Boeuf, which begins at the river and swings around behind the town to join Lake Palourde and complete the watery circle. It must be a brave town to flourish on such a low, unstable foundation, threatened by floods on the Atchafalaya and by winds from the Gulf; yet we found the inhabitants going about their affairs with no apparent concern about high tides and hurricanes. It reminded us of the old man living behind a Mississippi River levee, who said, when we asked him how he felt with the river higher than the land, "We don't pay any mind to it."

Morgan City, to us, seemed a little less French, more cosmopolitan, than other towns in southern Louisiana. Perhaps this is part of its seaport character. Though there is no deep-sea shipping, the wide river looks like an arm of the ocean, and many small salt-water vessels tie up at the line of docks which might be said to form one side of the principal street. We had much pleasure in sauntering along the waterfront, looking at the trawlers, tugs and oil company boats, one of which was an old LST (Landing Ship, Tank) being converted for some use, probably offshore drilling. The Coast Guard has a river dock, a whitened shell-

grinding plant stands at the mouth of Bayou Boeuf, and scattered along the shore are marine ways, boat builders, machine shops, net makers, a propeller works, and docks where boats stop for gasoline, oil, and ice.

Yet Morgan City has the feel of a river town, and the buildings which face the water there would not be out of place in a small city on the Ohio River—Maysville, Kentucky, perhaps. The muddy current of the Atchafalaya bearing driftwood toward the sea is a true river. Fresh-water fishermen live on shantyboats, and river towboats following the Intracoastal are often seen.

We found an old friend from the Ohio River moored in some backwater—the Light Tender *Greenbrier*, a steam stern-wheeler with the lines of a packet. The *Greenbrier* had made several stops at Four Mile Bar Light while we were at Brent, Kentucky, but was now apparently out of service. Many river boats make their final port in the brackish waters of southern Louisiana. Besides the *Amos K. Gordon* rusting in the swamp, we had seen the *Jack Rathbone* at Harvey, partly dismantled, its paddle wheel out on the bank. The *Rathbone* was a modern steel towboat which not many years before I had seen making its trial run on the upper Ohio.

Bayou Shaffer, where our shantyboat lay, had much about it which reminded us of rivers. We gathered dry driftwood along its shore, enjoying its quick, clean burning after the wet and sappy wood of the forest. This bayou is in reality a branch of the Atchafalaya, to which it is connected at both ends—the northern through Bayou Boeuf, the southern through Sweetbay Lake. When the Atchafalaya is in flood, these connecting bayous overflow their banks, too. Our friends back on Bayou Chene had told us of floods there. Thus the muddy water of the Mississippi seeps from one stream to another until it extends far back where one would never expect it to be; and far out into the Gulf, forming a wide band of copper between the shore and the blue sea water beyond.

Like the river water, river people find their way into these streams. We became acquainted with one on Bayou Shaffer, a lonely man, friendly and kindhearted—he helped me with our engine, which was cranky, and gave us a mess of crabs that he might have sold. Like others from the north, he was not quite happy in these southern waters; but it is a long, hard way back upstream, and the winters are cold up there.

This man lived on a small boat which was within our view down Bayou Shaffer. One morning he moved his tiny fleet away from the bank and headed south toward his winter harbor. We never saw him again.

This contact was typical of many we made along the waterways with river people whose course crossed ours; a brief period of intimacy which ended abruptly when they or we moved on. Quite different was the friendship established at Morgan City between L.T. Ozio and ourselves.

Immediately after our arrival in Bayou Shaffer, I set off in the skiff in search of drinking water. The dogs always jumped into the boat when they saw me preparing to start the engine, both of them crowding into the prow and trying to stand at its very point. This time Skipper had the choice position all for herself. Sambo was off in the woods hunting, but he must have heard the skiff engine and followed along shore as far as he could, for I happened to look back after we reached the Intracoastal and saw him swimming after us, his black head a mere spot on the broad stream. Swinging the skiff around in the wide circle which it required, I picked up Sambo, who shook water all over me and jumped happily into the bow beside Skipper.

I first asked for water at the ferry landing, where I was advised by the ferryman to go down the canal in the direction of Morgan City to Tom's Fish Dock. This I found to be a rambling waterside structure—packing house and fish dock combined—to which both fresh and salt water fishermen brought their catch. River catfish, buffalo, goo, or frogs might be received from one boat, while another, in from the Gulf, would be unloading crabs, shrimp or turtles.

It chanced that I met there a young man who introduced himself as L.T. Ozio—a Spanish name, he said—who was engaged in this business with his father. While the water cans and jugs were filling, our conversation quickly passed over the ordinary and ranged into topics which had no connection with shantyboating or fish buying. One never knows where a lover of the arts will be met with, or when or under what guise an artist will appear. It is well to be prepared and open-minded.

On another evening I went to the fish dock with the skiff and brought L.T. to our boat. It was, I think, a memorable experience for us all—the ride on the wide bayou as the sun was setting, our shantyboat, the paintings which I had to show, and our friend's sympathetic response.

The next and last time we saw L.T. was on the day we pulled out of Bayou Shaffer. He was a little surprised to see us abroad on such a windy day, but we had not the benefit of radio. It had seemed a moderate wind from the south when we left our mooring, just what we wanted to help us on the upstream run; for our plan was to go up the Atchafalaya past Morgan City to the mouth of Bayou Teche, which would be our route westward.

When we reached Bayou Boeuf that morning the full force of the wind was felt. Tom's Fish Dock was on a lee shore, a tricky landing which we made neatly. It was a busy day on the dock and we had little chance to visit. After watching briefly the large-scale preparation of fish and crabs, taking on all the drinking water that could be carried, and receiving as a parting gift some large catfish heads for the dogs, we began our struggle with the wind.

It was possible to pull away from the dock, though directly into the wind, but when we tried to turn westward the wind carried us back toward shore. With engine running at full speed, the best we could do was to hold our position. I hailed a passing motorboat and asked for a tow, but the man said he must first take his fish to the dock.

Anna was steering from the skiff and doing a nice job of it. The wind did not lessen but it must have shifted its direction a few points, for suddenly Anna was able to turn the boat slightly to the west without losing ground. Though still headed almost south, we sailed westward and soon had the satisfaction of rounding the point into the river.

Here we parted company with the Intracoastal Waterway, which crossed the river at a downstream angle before continuing west as a canal. Our course was directly upstream, and with the wind astern now, we rolled along.

Almost at once we were faced with a new difficulty. The Southern Pacific Railroad bridge just ahead of us was so close to the water that it was doubtful if we could pass under it. There was a swing span over near the other shore but it would be hazardous to cross the wide river in the trough of the midstream waves. As we neared the bridge I sighted along the roof of the pitching boat as best I could. There was a chance we might slip under. Anna steered straight ahead and I climbed to the roof with wire cutters, ready to clip the guy wires of the chimneys. This was not necessary, but I had to duck my head when passing under the bridge, though standing on the lower part of the roof. If we had not been moving so fast I could have shaken hands with the railroad man who passed just at that moment on his motor car.

We now sailed along the Morgan City waterfront, running free with the wind and waves, the sound of the skiff engine popping behind almost lost in the uproar. We picked out landmarks seen in our walks along shore, and guessed that the triangular red flag fluttering in the wind was a storm warning.

At the upper end of town the highway crosses the river on a three-span bridge with a high clearance. When we had passed under this we made for the other side, diagonally, running for the mouth of Bayou Teche. The waves became higher in midriver. Whitecaps broke around us. I had to ride in the stern of the skiff to hold the propeller under water. The shantyboat pitched and jerked so violently that I expected the lines to part. The painter of the johnboat did break two strands, but luckily I saw it in time. Any manoeuvering out there would have been risky; it was all we could do to hold a straight course.

As we closed with the western shore, the water became smoother, though the winds continued. Just before turning in to Bayou Teche, I looked upstream for the last time and suddenly felt a desire to go on up the river, the course of which was marked by low points and headlands until lost in the forest. This longing was due in part to the old urge to go upriver, which I had felt as long as I could remember; it came also from the thought that I could follow this river upstream and after many winding miles gain those upper reaches and hills which will always be home to me, and which at that moment seemed so far away.

VIII

The entrance to Bayou Teche can be located from a distance by a concrete-and-steel flood gate. This gate is a small unit in an extensive system of works whose purpose is to ease the strain on the levees of the Mississippi River during a flood by making a safety valve of the Atchafalaya. The volume of water diverted from the Mississippi will lower the crest on that river and lessen the danger at New Orleans, but it will cause abnormally high stages on the Atchafalaya. To meet this danger, new and higher levees are being built along that stream, and its tributaries will be protected from flood waters by gates such as the one we had just reached at the mouth of Teche.

    This stark, modern structure at the very entrance to the celebrated Bayou Teche might be disconcerting to the sentimental traveler whose mind was filled with the legends and history of the most romantic of the Louisiana bayous. As for ourselves, we approached with an open mind, tempering our expectations with the remembrance of past disappointments in places which are rated highly, prepared to see the stream and country as they are today; and if highways, oil wells, and standardized living should be found, to admit the fact and not pretend that all was exotic quaintness; although there is a tendency, if one loves a wagon and a steamboat more than an automobile or a diesel tug, to cherish old ways and relics of the past and to leave out of the picture much of today.

For another reason our record would not be extensive or complete. Though we sailed a long way through the Teche country and lived there four months, we do not claim to have made a thorough study of it. We did not go out of our way to meet people who lived there, or try to see everything. Perhaps only offhand or casual observations can be expected from such a voyage as ours, of which the essence is to be at home while traveling. To a shantyboater, the places and people along the way are often no more than a background to his intimate round of living.

Leaving the Atchafalaya on this windy day, we chugged through a narrow passage between high concrete walls, at the ends of which were open steel gates. The walls were deserted now, but in times of high water the gates will be manned, and boats entering or leaving Teche will be locked through.

Beyond the gates the bayou was about as wide as a small river, the Cumberland perhaps. Trees lined the grassy shores, graceful willows and feathery cypress contrasting with the dense roundness of the live oaks. Farmhouses and russet fields showed through the openings as we sailed along.

That day's run was brought to an abrupt end at the first turn to the south by the wind, which still blew across the flat country. We were in an awkward spot, on the outside of a bend, in water so shallow that the boat could not be moored to the bank. This condition was a bother along the whole course of Bayou Teche. Luckily there is little heavy traffic, but on this evening a procession of fishing boats passed, all going west—*Ramos Ace, Butch, Mercedes, Santa Maria, Three Brothers, The Kind Father,* and a dozen others. Most of them slowed down, but the few that passed at full speed gave us a shaking up, with the shantyboat nearly resting on the bottom.

We left at daybreak and soon passed the town of Patterson on the left bank, the port to which the fishing boats were returning for the weekend. It was a rather long run from the coast in to the harbor, but in this country the towns must be built inland in order to have a firm, dry foundation and access to a road.

In spite of its prosaic name, Patterson was a picturesque town, with its docks along the narrow bayou, the trawlers now lying three abreast. There was a small shipyard and the usual assortment of sheds, landings and skiffs that make these small harbors so fascinating. On the country side of the bayou lay some abandoned hulls with clipper bows, which had once carried masts and sails. We often wondered about sailing on the bayous. The wind could be depended on in that flat country, but on the crooked streams only short reaches could be sailed, with much poling in between. Sailing was so completely in the past that no one ever mentioned it, and the old hulls, if still serviceable, had been converted to power.

The bridge above Patterson was not shown on our maps. Since it looked too low for us to pass under, I blew three blasts for an opening. Even with the engine throttled down we almost got too close to it, the wind carrying us on. The bridge tender came running out, "*Ça ne prendra pas longtemps.*" He signaled a passing truck to lower the boom on the far side and began to open the bridge by walking round and round a capstan in the center. There was just space for us to slip through when we came up. This was lucky, for it is awkward to stop our fleet, having no reverse gear. The only way to check forward motion is by poles, or by running into the bank.

Not far beyond Patterson the bayou turns toward the north and widens. Here on the inside of a bend we were able to work the boat in against a solid bank. Mossy live oaks branched overhead, their buttressed roots reaching to the water. When a plank had been laid from the deck to a level root and a little clearing done on shore, we were at home.

There was much to interest us at this station. To the north was a levee and a little settlement of campboats and cabins, the boats lying in a pond half filled with hyacinths. On the levee were a few rough buildings, one of which was a store, though not much larger than a family pantry. Part of its trade came from people living beyond the levee in that wild and mysterious region of lakes and bayous with names like Bayou Boutte, Lake Chicot, or Bayou L'Embarras. Primarily fishermen and trappers, they were of an independent race that was said to scorn the benefits of Social Security. They are apparently becoming reconciled to the new order, however, for they are giving up fishing to work

on levee construction, abandoning their boats for cabins on the made ground, and moving closer to towns so that their children can go to school. A boatload of eight or ten varied youngsters passed us every morning on their way to meet a school bus on the highway, returning in the afternoon. Evidently the mothers pooled their children, for each day a different lady was rowing expertly at the stand-up oars of the pushing skiff. Sometimes on the return trip one of the children—having begged for the honor, no doubt—was at the heavy oars, though they could hardly be reached by short arms.

Our neighbors visited us, out of friendliness and curiosity. All were French, even Mrs. Wilson, who was of the Simoneau family. Some names sounding like "Mo" and "So" were hard to understand, and the Cajuns themselves often could not spell them.

We admired these people who lived so close to the wilderness, perhaps even envied them a little. They told us much that was helpful, and when I tried fishing with what they called bush lines, I did well. It was a novelty to us to catch fish on hooks in December. A real bush-line fisherman sets up a row of poles in the mud parallel to the shore and in deep enough water. A short string with a single hook is tied to each pole. It is more fun than fishing with a trot line on the bottom, for you can see at a distance when you have a fish by the shaking of the pole. If it is a big fish the pole sways back and forth and you hurry to it hoping to get there before he breaks loose. Most of them are catfish, just like the river cats for all we could see. One blue cat weighed eleven pounds. Small fish were used for bait. These I caught in the cast net, sometimes drawing it up spangled with silvery shad, or "sardines."

Fresh vegetables to go with our fish came from a field across the bayou, a sort of winter truck patch planted between the long rows of new cane. We picked a few turnips here and there, or beets or carrots, and now and then a mess of spinach or mustard. Peas were beginning to bloom.

In the middle of the field stood an old wooden house, long abandoned but erect and straight, with a brick chimney in the center having a fireplace facing each of the two rooms. On another shore were some curious mounds in a grove of magnificent live oaks.

The shore about our landing was mostly open with brushy thickets, a fine place for birds. Meadowlarks were singing, there were mockingbirds, shrikes (which at first we mistook for mockingbirds), towhees, cardinals, thrashers, and the redwings and grackles which are everywhere in this low country. A bird new to us was the vermilion flycatcher. Sometimes a flock of wood ibises flew over in two or three lines, alternately flapping and sailing, continuing their serene way regardless of gunfire from the campboats.

The weather gave variety to the succession of days. On our arrival it was so sunny and warm that I went without a shirt. Sudden heavy rains came up from the south, often at night, with lightning, thunder and wind. We would close the shutters in time, if possible, let in the dogs, mop up the drips, and bail out the skiff lest rainwater get into the engine. One morning the wind shifted to northwest and brought weather cold enough to

freeze the banana trees and the remnant of mosquitoes. We eagerly breathed the crisp air. Fires of dead branches from live oaks burned in both stove and fireplace, and for a day or two the children from the campboats stayed home from school. The cold wind soon blew itself out, and the sweet, balmy south wind returned—also some of the mosquitoes.

We made two or three trips back to Patterson in the skiff. It was a small, comfortable place with old frame buildings overshadowed by live oaks, but the effect was somewhat spoiled by having U.S. 90 on its main street. The waterfront of the town, as is always the case, was the most interesting part.

One day we mailed our Christmas cards, one hundred seventy-five of them in a bunch. We had hoped to have them postmarked by a French name, but it chanced to be Patterson. The making of the woodblock print for these cards, the printing, mounting, and attendant writing had taken up much of the recent days. All of the work was a pleasure to do and it brought our friends closer to us.

It was at this station that Skipper had the next litter of pups, only two, and so small that they had to be taught to eat. They soon picked up, and their early life was more comfortable than that of the last batch in midsummer. In a few days their mother was out chasing rabbits with Sambo.

This was the only place on Bayou Teche that gave us an expanse of water to look over. It was caused partly by the junction of two streams, and we learned with surprise, from our neighbors and from a close study of the excellent U.S.E.D. maps, that the stream coming in from the west was Bayou Teche, and that the one we had followed up from the Atchafalaya thus far was not Bayou Teche, as we had supposed, but the Lower Atchafalaya, a side channel of the main river. At this point the Lower Atchafalaya turned north, but its connection with the main river was cut off by a levee built right across from bank to bank. Thus there is no longer a Lower Atchafalaya River, and the section once called by that name is now considered to be part of Bayou Teche.

The levee across the river is not new and is constantly settling into the soft river bed. The construction now in progress was raising the levee to its full height. The work went on through most of the night in fair weather, and the noise and lights bothered us. We consoled ourselves by thinking how much this employment meant to the river people, and by remembering that we would soon be moving on.

It was a bright, cool morning when we cast off and waved for the last time at the boatload of school children. Soon we were moving up Bayou Teche, our interest in the passing shores and in the places which lay ahead of us. The bayou was narrower now, not much wider than a broad street. It wound in gentle curves through sugar cane country, and from our deck we watched the harvest which in these extensive fields is all done by machinery. High-wheeled carts were used to haul the cane, and two or three of these in line behind a tractor crossing a bridge ahead of us resembled a giant toy train, the effect being more real if the tractor smoked a little.

Many bridges crossed the bayou. If it were a side road or a private road to a sugarhouse, the bridge was likely to be an old wooden structure, braced and guyed, each differing from the next as if they had been designed and made by local builders who had worked out their own ideas. Some were pontoon bridges, a single barge across the stream, but most were of the swinging type, pivoting in the center. They were turned slowly by means of a long-handled capstan around which a man or two slowly walked and pushed. Perhaps a man's wife might help him or even do the job by herself. The bridge tender, often a Negro, might not appear until after we had blown our horn several times; or he might see us coming and have the bridge open for us, but never more than would allow us to squeeze through.

Not far up the Teche we crossed the Wax Lake Outlet, one of the canals from the Atchafalaya to the Gulf through which flood water will be drained off. It flowed with a slow current now but it must be a millrace when the rivers are full. In such times the steel gates across Teche at each side of the canal will be closed and boats will have to use the locks near Morgan City.

Formerly Teche and the Atchafalaya were connected by several natural channels. It was through one of these that Evangeline's boat made its way to the upper Teche, having turned off the Mississippi and come down the Atchafalaya, which when it passes through Grand Lake is close to the bayou. At one point we tied up our fleet and rowed in the johnboat out a narrow canal to the Grand Lake levee, from the top of which we looked over the wide water to the north. Cypress Island, lying close to the far shore, separated Six Mile Lake to the east from Grand Lake, which extended westward as far as we could see. On the near shore a path led down among the trees to a fisherman's landing where boats were pulled out and nets, floats, traps, tarring vat and other gear lay scattered about. From this prospect of open water we returned with some regret to the narrow bayou and its cultivated shores; yet even there we were conscious of the separation of water from land, and of the integrity of the bayou. No stream, however small, is landlocked.

We voyaged on, past plantations, through bridges, now in the back country, now with a highway along the shore. A large sugarhouse was passed, its brick buildings as ancient as the unpainted cabins. Farther along was a busy sawmill, running full blast with much noise and spouting steam. Barges piled with logs lay at the foot of an incline leading to the whining saws.

Before reaching the city of Franklin we halted at the narrow entrance to the lock of the Hanson Canal, which runs southward from Bayou Teche, to find out if we could pass this way in case the flood gates on Teche should be closed. The lockman assured us that the canal was always navigable to the Intracoastal.

Franklin makes a good impression on the chance traveler who approaches by water. It looked so much like a river town that we could imagine we were aboard one of the old Teche steamboats. The landing is an open, grassy square before the courthouse, and the town lies on high ground, for that country, the streets sloping upward somewhat like the grade from a river. With only a brief stop for drinking water we continued up the bayou, past some old houses in gardens and groves, past another sawmill, this one idle, another sugarhouse, another bridge. When in open country again we looked for a place to tie up. As usual it was hard to find deep enough water along the shore, but this time we solved the problem by mooring the shantyboat abreast an abandoned float which lay on the bottom near the bank. One plank was placed from deck to float, another from float to shore, which was a strip of bushy wilderness with cane fields beyond. There were no houses close to us, no road on either side of the bayou.

It is hard to explain why one tarries at a certain place. This landing had little to recommend it, yet we remained there forty

days. It was a serene, contented time for us; the unmarred days flowed smoothly one into another.

On many of them the warm sun rose and set clear, and the tawny-shored bayou, unruffled by a breath of wind, was of a more intense blue than the sky. There were dark days, too, when rain came in a misty drizzle, and we went about our indoor work before a cheerful fire. In all weather we found much to do, but work and pastime were inseparable.

Christmas came a few days after our arrival and was duly celebrated. Our Christmas tree was a small live oak from the pasture across the bayou, so dwarfed and cow-bitten that it resembled a miniature tree from a Japanese garden. We found some mistletoe—rare in that section—growing in a mock orange tree—a rare tree, too, and an unusual host for mistletoe. Cypress knees made attractive candlesticks. Some of the wrinkled and twisted pieces, like stalagmites, suggested living forms and might have been fashioned by a modern sculptor; one in particular we called the Madonna.

The two pups added a playful touch. One was thoroughly a hound, the other a typical Skipper pup—small, black and white, short-haired.

There was much to remind us that it was a southern Christmas; fireworks in the distance for one thing, and the warm sun. On Christmas day we swam in the bayou, briefly. The year ended, however, with a touch of winter that froze ice on the water bucket on deck.

Firewood was scarce about our landing. I ranged along the shores with the johnboat, picking up dead branches and driftwood, which is never entirely lacking on any waterway. Live oak was the hottest-burning wood. Sometimes I came upon the ashes and charred stumps of huge oaks left by charcoal burners who had worked at their ancient and poetic craft throughout the South before gas came to be almost universally used for heating and cooking.

One day when I was foraging down the bayou on the far side I met two boys out hunting with a Christmas rifle. They returned to the boat with me and in time became frequent visitors. Named Faucheux, they lived in Oak Bluff Plantation, which was situated on the bayou to the eastward. The plantation bell was often heard but the buildings were hidden in a grove of oaks and pecans—the pecans along Teche are so mossy that they make almost as dense a screen as the evergreen oaks. We went to Oak Bluff one day at the boys' invitation. The great frame building was aged and weathered but it had an air of elegance and dignity more convincing than the old houses which are "restored." We admired the balance and grace of its proportions, the skillful workmanship of the craftsmen who built it. The Faucheux family lived in as many rooms as they needed. To live now in a building designed for the abundant and spacious days of the Old South presents many difficulties; yet such an expansive habitation must be inspiring. Think of the boxes which the race of men are putting together nowadays. We wondered how our tiny boat impressed Mrs. Faucheux when she visited us.

This plantation belonged to a sugar company for which Mr. Faucheux managed the cane growing. Huge, unearthly machines were being used for harvesting. The last of the crop had been frozen and was fit only for molasses. The Negro hands lived in the old slave quarters, a row of bare cottages somewhat like the company houses in a coal-mining town, without the shroud of soot. In the smokeless, rain-washed air of Louisiana the old brick chimneys were red as if new.

The only other contacts we had with people in this place were casual ones in Franklin. It was a pleasant town where it always seemed to be summer, perhaps because of the streets shaded with live oaks, and because we went only on sunny days. Franklin supplied all of our wants except wheat, which is out of the question in Louisiana. Rice in a natural state was not to be had, although we saw pumps and flumes for watering rice fields along Bayou Teche. So we fell back on hen scratch, a mixture of grain sorghum, wheat, corn and what-not, which may have more virtues than wheat alone. I ground it into flour for Anna's baking, toasted and ground it for a breakfast stir-about. The dogs had their share cooked with fish heads and greens.

Green vegetables came from the Franklin stores, since it was not garden country about our landing. We often got a quantity of trimmings to be used as greens for the dogs; yet we cooked the best parts for ourselves. The outside leaves of cauliflower make a tasty dish, and being green are probably better for you than the bleached heads.

Another item we sought in Franklin stores was blackstrap molasses. Our experience with natural rice—and with soybeans in Kentucky—was repeated: products not in common use are hard to get even in a district where they originate. One day we stopped at the sugarhouse to ask for blackstrap and were generously given several quarts. It was not true blackstrap, however, but molasses made from frozen cane. Blackstrap, as we understand it, is made from the cane after the sugar has been extracted.

I did very well on bush lines here and soon had enough catfish to make a smokehouse worth while. I contrived one out of a couple of old tubs and scraps of sheet metal from a dump, and smoked fish for the coming voyage.

Shantyboats along the rivers often have small floating docks, made perhaps of salvaged timbers or logs, or planks fastened to oil drums. On the bayous, with little rise or fall to the water, a dock can be a fixed affair. In all cases they are put to good use since they afford a clean, level floor for working and a handy place to keep all sorts of truck; and when high water overflows the shore, the chicken coop or pigpen can be moved onto the dock, and firewood cut there. We had always thought how nice it would be to have a dock, but this one on Bayou Teche near Franklin was our first. We found it even more useful than we had anticipated. It was like an extension of the deck. On washdays I stretched the clothesline back and forth from poles set up at the corners of the dock—a great advantage since there was no opening on the brushy, uneven shore. We also pulled the skiff out on the dock to give the bottom another coating of copper paint. By waiting for a high tide the hauling out and launching were made easy.

This unbroken succession of serene days encouraged painting and writing. I wrote in the log every day, which was well, for otherwise we would have lost track of the days of the week. Here is the entry for January 4, 1951.

> This is the warmest, sunniest birthday that I can remember. We ate dinner on deck, arms bare and almost too warm in the sun. What did I do today? Nothing that I would not have done yesterday or might not do tomorrow, although Anna's love and attention set this day apart; yet even that is my daily lot. I did some writing this morning after the chores were taken care of, sitting on the bank in the sun with the pups, who remained out there until the sun was low.
>
> Immediately after dinner—roast beef from Franklin, browned potatoes and carrots, the Galiano jar of corn, peaches and a piece of birthday cake—I set up my easel. Later we played together and then it was time for the evening roundup. We all went out in the johnboat to cast, but caught very little. Now I sit by the fire writing this while Anna prepares supper. Yesterday's delayed Christmas mail came on an appropriate day since it brought four or five packages beside sixty-odd Christmas cards.
>
> I am fifty-one years old today. As I was painting I felt that what I could do, what I could see and how I could express it were worth even longer years of living. My writing is an unknown factor but it may amount to something. It is another expression of what I have felt

and lived for. The creation of an environment in which it is possible to do this work, which allows the necessary time and freedom, peace of mind, happiness and security—this in itself is a success which is not always achieved.

To mark the day the bayou flowed westward for the first time, the water rose to a higher level. A new evening star low in the sky shone brightly just after sunset.

It was near the end of January on a Sunday that we lined up our boats and moved away from the dock. Passing Oak Bluff Plantation I repeated to Anna a story told me by the Faucheux boy, that the present building replaced an older one which had been destroyed or torn down because it was in the line of fire of Confederate gunboats on the Teche during the Civil War, firing on boats out on Grand Lake!

We soon passed another plantation, Oak Lawn, a pretentious, ornate mansion whose lawn extends to the bayou shore, where a little summer house has been built on a pier. Years later we chanced to hear something of the history of Oak Lawn. In its day one of the most splendid plantation houses in the South, it was later acquired by an enterprising towboat captain, a man from the North who, when he had first seen the mansion from the deck of his small steamboat, had said, "Some day I will own that place." He was able to realize this ambition when he struck it rich in the Teche oil field, but before he had time to get much pleasure from his new possession it burned to the ground. Apparently the captain was not at all discouraged for he rebuilt Oak Lawn after its original plan, with some modern improvements. Now the plantation is in another phase of its history; the splendor of the great house is tarnished, and the grounds and the little pavilion on the dock are neglected.

The riverman who had owned Oak Lawn was from the Ohio River, and this tale is one of the many told by his cousin. The two of them began their river careers together as small boys on their uncle's trading boat.

After a short run, for which we took two days, the Charenton Canal was reached. This would have led us back to the Intracoastal, but we chose to keep on Bayou Teche and explore its upper reaches. Before proceeding, however, we lay by for a few days to wait out a spell of cold weather. During this time the shantyboat was moored in deep water along the shore of an island formed by two entrances to the canal. The branches of live oaks which spread over the water were so massive that we made sure they were sound before pulling our boat under them. Although the island was small, the dogs discovered a rabbit there, which they chased round and round until it was forced to take to the water. It swam across the bayou and through a cypress swamp to some fields where later the dogs picked up the trail and continued the hunt.

The Southern Pacific crossed the canal near enough for us to enjoy seeing the trains. Sometimes a splendid streamliner came to a stop when the bridge happened to be open for a passing boat—it might be the tug *Jupiter* with covered barges of sugar, on its circuitous voyage to Lafourche; or the small *Norma Webb* of Houston, a boat we were to see often on the upper Teche. Once our old friend *Mary-Joan* came through with a barge of shells. There appeared to be more traffic on that part of the bayou which lay ahead of us.

Westward of our position, across the canal, was the little town of Baldwin. We walked there one frigid day, the coldest of the winter; eighteen degrees, they said, and it felt like zero, with a stiff wind from the north and a skift of snow on the ground. A Negro couple we met on the road took a fancy to the black and white puppy and asked for him, saying he would be their yard dog. We felt sure he would have a good home. The hound pup had already found a place for himself with the Theriot boy at Oak Bluff. As always we missed the lively pups when they were gone.

The cold was soon replaced by warm, sunny weather from the south, and we resumed our course up Bayou Teche. A still narrower stream, it traversed a pleasant rural country where the farms were smaller. Low levees appeared, and as we pushed slowly on against a steady current, the bayou seemed to be coming to life and changing into a river. The current was from Grand Lake, this section of Teche being part of the Charenton drainage system. It was almost too much for our feeble power at a certain railroad bridge where the channel had been narrowed and made shallow by a rock fill. We had been warned of this place. We had been told, too, that the bridge was always open. It was closed this time, but a young Negro came out at our approach and began turning the steel span to let us through. We made a run at it but could not buck the current that poured out between the piers. I ran a line to the middle pier with the johnboat, and the strength of our arms combined with that of the engine brought our heavy boat up to the bridge. Holding it there I carried another line to the upper end of the piling above the bridge, and we began to inch through the opening.

Meanwhile the bridge tender, who had been anxiously looking down the track, shouted to us that the train was coming and that we must get out of there so he could close the bridge. I was determined not to lose what we had gained, but it was doubtful that we could make it through. The Negro boy became really excited now, waving his arms and pointing to the approaching train. Seeing that we were not going to back up, he began to close the bridge behind us. The locomotive came to a stop overhead and stood puffing while we labored. In the nick of time an unexpected push was received from a small skiff which happened along at that moment. Our boat cleared the bridge, the span was closed, the train crossed; then the bridge was opened and the Negro silently departed. The train was only a small cut of freight cars and surely in no hurry. It makes a daily run across the bridge, which is left closed until the train returns a few hours later—unless a boat happens along. We had come at an awkward interval, but it was over now. The current at the end of the piling was easy enough to allow us to proceed normally.

The man in the skiff who had helped us said that this place was much worse at times. Not long before, a boat like ours in attempting to drift down through the bridge had struck one of the piers and capsized, and those on board were drowned.

Above the bridge, the Charenton Canal turns off to the right toward Grand Lake, and beyond that point the bayou resumes its sluggish way, bending toward the southwest until it picks up the main drag; then it runs northwest in an almost straight line, with highway and railroad along one side. Both shores are considerably built up and bridges are frequent. We ran slowly along, that rainy afternoon, looking for a mooring place that would not be in someone's back yard. By evening we were less particular, and a mile beyond Jeanerette landed in back of a sugarhouse. Since it was not operating, the place was quiet and secluded.

The rain ceased during the night and by morning a head wind was blowing. We decided to lay over and do a washing, a decision which was encouraged by a little pond of rain water nearby and an open space convenient for hanging out the clothes. We were quite pleased with ourselves for managing a washing en route.

In the past few days the skiff engine, which had never run perfectly, had taken a turn for the worse. It was hard to start and it missed badly. We managed to get away from the sugarhouse, but on that day's run the engine failed completely. Though I tried all I could think of, I could not get a pop out of it.

Scouting about for help, I talked to some Negroes who lived in pretty cabins across the bayou, and visited the Department of Agriculture station near which we had made our forced landing. Somewhere the idea came up that the ignition coil might be dead. Next day I took the bicycle down from the roof and pedaled to New Iberia, a few miles farther on. The ride along the level road was pleasant, and after so much boating it was like flying to ride a bicycle. I was struck by the insignificance of the bayou when seen from a landsman's viewpoint. The scanty line of trees that marked its course might have been along a ditch; yet when we were on it, the bayou seemed spacious and free, the center of the universe.

New Iberia is the largest place on Bayou Teche. At the Ford agency there, Leblanc and Broussard, I was lucky to obtain a Model T spark coil. In this transaction I described our engine as five horse power, one cylinder; and wondered what the parts clerk and others were laughing at—I had forgotten to say it was in a boat.

It may or may not have been because of the new coil, but next morning the engine started and ran fairly well. We cruised right through the middle of New Iberia—business district on the left, residences on the right, with bridges between the two parts. Rounding a half-circle bend beyond the town, we found a harbor near another sugarhouse. Farther on was open country, but the opposite shore was built up with new suburban houses whose lawns and gardens sloped gently to the bayou.

A Sunday followed. Its influence was more strongly felt in this inhabited place, and we kept the day conventionally, to some extent. The watchman from the sugarhouse paid us a visit, greeting us first in French but changing to a formal English for our benefit. We learned that the sugarhouse had ceased operations but was pumping blackstrap into tank cars. Observing the interest this raised in us, the watchman promised us some blackstrap and later came back with a gallon in an open can. Anna at once made a pan of gingerbread.

We found many ways to use blackstrap. It has an affinity for canned milk and this makes it very good on our whole grain cooked cereal. A spoonful of blackstrap in a glass of diluted condensed milk makes an excellent drink, and Anna sweetens several kinds of bread with blackstrap.

On Monday morning we went into New Iberia, a town which gave us the impression of being strongly French. Some of the villas along the bayou had names like Le Beau Soleil, Chez Nous, Le Beau Rêve, and the store names were French. One of them—Duplanti's—was a welcome change from the standardized chain store, although in the smaller places even the chain stores become more local and individual. Duplanti's was primarily a feed store, a barnlike place where all sorts of groceries and merchandise were scattered about in heaps, stacks, and open cartons. The customers, dodging hand trucks of feed being wheeled in or out, picked up what they wanted and carried it to an elevated

wire cage in the center of the store from which Mr. Duplanti could keep an eye on everything while he totaled up the bill and made change. A Negro boy weighed feed to order. We bought some pigeon feed, a mixture of kaffir corn, dry peas, black-seeded vetch, and other things, as a change from hen scratch; also soybeans, a black variety which gave Anna's salads and bread a new look.

On the afternoon of the same day we departed up the bayou, which ran eastward for five miles, then swung around on its true course to the northwest. A definite change had come over Bayou Teche. It was flowing with a steady current, slow, but always in one direction; it was narrower and not so shallow along the edge; its shores often sloped up to grassy knolls. We were ascending a river.

There were still some level cane fields and plantations, but many small farms and cottages reminded us of Bayou Lafourche. Some of these Cajun homesteads, gray with age, were so close to the shore that we could study them in detail as we moved slowly by. The yard might be surrounded by a fence of hand-hewn cypress pickets. The houses usually had porches or galleries on the long sides which the low, sweeping roof overhung with unbroken lines. The square porch columns, and sometimes a front door with overhead and side lights, gave an air of dignity to the smallest houses. The small-paned windows had solid wooden shutters. A most unusual feature was a narrow stairway on the porch, from its outer edge up into the attic. The door at the top must have been quite low, but this would not inconvenience the boys of the family who slept in the attic—the *garçonnière*.

At this time two small tugs were making regular trips on the upper Teche—*Dart* and *Norma Webb*. They towed an oil barge or two, empty going up, loaded on the down trip, probably with crude oil from the wells at the head of Teche. Because of the narrowness of the stream the boats passed us carefully, and slowly enough to allow a little conversation. They ran to Port Arthur, Texas, and went through twenty-six bridges and passed four cable ferries on the way. The captain would sometimes inform us where the other boat was and when we could expect to meet it. Only once did we come near to collision, and then it was my fault. When I pulled in to the bank to get out of the way I made fast only one end of our boat. The suction of the passing tow pulled the other end out into the channel, where the barge just grazed by.

This section of Bayou Teche was so crooked that we could not be sure, when the sound of a boat was heard, whether it would overtake or meet us. The stream carried us through a sylvan country of small and infrequent rural towns. At one of the bridges we stopped to get gasoline and water from a neat country store which stood beside the road above. The proprietor, a merry Cajun, was amazed that a boat from Kentucky—pronounced by him with a French twist—should have penetrated this far.

Then we entered a rough, wild reach where the narrow bayou was closed in by high banks. Proceeding slowly against the swifter current, we heard a well-known sound—the roar of water pouring over a dam. Soon we saw the dam, the white water underneath it, and on the left bank a stone-built lock. This made a river of the Teche without a doubt; it might have been the Green River in Kentucky.

After I had blown the customary long and short on our horn, a head appeared over the top of the wall and the familiar procedure of locking followed. This was the Keystone Lock and Dam, the only one on Teche, with a lift of about six feet. We talked with the lockmaster, "Happy," about our plan of going on up Teche to the Ruth Canal and passing through it into Bayou Vermilion or Vermilion River. Happy said it could no longer be done because of a flood control gate across the canal; so our papers were made out, "Brent to St. Martinville, Louisiana." We made our way to that port, four or five miles farther upstream, finding almost no current above the lock. The shores were lower and lined with the tall yellow grass of the marsh.

Reaching St. Martinville we landed at the famous Evangeline oak to get our bearings before pushing on a short distance to a mooring place suggested by Happy. St. Martinville is said to be the town to which Evangeline came in her search for Gabriel, her Acadian lover. The tourist is reminded of this story at every turn, and a tablet marks the spreading live oak at the landing where Evangeline first stepped ashore. The bayou shore underneath the oak is a smooth lawn, and near the water stands an old brick schoolhouse which had been an inn when steamboats ran on Bayou Teche.

The bridge just above was our present concern. No one answered our blasts on the horn except a small boy on the shore who said the bridge tender lived up town. I aimed the horn that way and blew again. The helpful boy said I could 'phone the tender from the nearby power house; then he shouted, "Here he comes." He looked more like the mayor of the town than the keeper of the bridge, such a dressed-up and important man. He asked when we would be coming back; in several days, I said. The siren whined three times, the bridge opened—by electric power, of course.

Not far above town we landed on the left bank in a small cove at the lower end of the Longfellow-Evangeline State Park. The bayou stretched on to the northwest, a narrow aisle between mossy trees; but this point, seventy-five miles from the Atchafalaya, was the limit of our voyage up Bayou Teche. I did go on sixteen or seventeen miles farther with Happy, the lockmaster, when he stopped at our boat on his way to the town of Breaux Bridge. He was in a government launch and his errand was to assist a photographer in taking an official picture from mid-bayou of the new bridge at Breaux Bridge. Since headquarters wanted a photograph of the bridge in a raised position, the bridge tender was to be the third member of the trio, but he failed to keep the appointment, dismayed no doubt by the rain; so the enterprise was postponed until fair weather. I was the only one to profit by the expedition. It gave me a chance to see more of Bayou Teche, and to see for myself the Ruth Canal. Happy was right—we could not have gotten through unless we could have made a portage.

Bayou Teche is navigable another fifteen miles beyond Breaux Bridge to Arnaudville, but few boats go that far. The bridges are opened only by appointment with the tender, who may live at a distance.

En route Happy entertained me with yarns of his river experiences. He was born near New Orleans, and the Mississippi River had a large part in his upbringing. He shipped on an ocean tanker when still in high school but later changed to river boats, some of them belonging to the U.S. Engineers. This led to appointments at different locks. I believe he knew every boat on the rivers.

He knew Bayou Teche, too. One story he told was of the Mayo brothers, who cruised the bayous in their own boat. They carried a stock of peppermint candy which they tossed to children along the shores. Their boat came to be known as "Le Bateau de Candy," the "candy boat."

The eleven days we lay here gave us a new kind of shantyboating. Being anchored in a park had many conveniences, such as drinking water from a hydrant nearby and plenty of picnic scraps for the dogs. We wandered through the park where the grass was already a fresh green, and visited the museum, an old mansion containing many articles, pictures and documents relating to French life on Bayou Teche. Of great interest to us was the Acadian Craft House where friendly Mrs. Daspit showed us examples of local handwork. This encouraged us to be on the watch for Acadians who still practiced their traditional arts, and later it pleased us to find a lady weaving on an old hand-made loom, forming patterns of white and brown cotton—she raised the cotton herself and called the brown kind nankeen.

On Saturdays and Sundays the park was well filled, and new names were added to our guest register. An official welcome was extended by Wade Martin, then Secretary of State of Louisiana, a native of the St. Martinville country. It was a pleasure to talk with him and his sister, Mrs. Guirard, whose book on St. Martinville history we had read. A group of St. Martinville high school girls brightened one afternoon. Though in holiday spirits, they were well-mannered and showed an intelligent interest in our long voyage and our way of life. Their French names, and a certain native inflection in speaking, gave them an added charm.

While I was writing at a park table a man with a camera introduced himself—Lewis Bernard of New Iberia, freelance photographer and journalist, who wanted to write an article about us. I told him that I was engaged at that very moment in doing so, but that he was welcome to try his hand at it. We saw Bernard—and Mrs. Bernard and their growing family—at different places within reach of New Iberia. What happened to his article is unknown to us, but some of the best photographs we have of our boat and of ourselves were taken by Lewis Bernard.

All this was shantyboating in style, far removed from the rough and muddy days we had often known on solitary riverbanks. We even hobnobbed with a cabin cruiser belonging to a St. Martinville doctor whose recreation was to navigate the bayou. He had made some long trips, too, and to hear him tell of White Lake and of that almost legendary *chênière*, Pecan Island, roused our desire to voyage into the endless marsh country to the southwest.

The town of St. Martinville was a friendly place where we always met with someone inclined to talk as we strolled about the tidy streets. A French differing from that of Bayou Lafourche was heard, so much nearer to what Anna was used to that she had hopes of understandng it. There was a touch of old France about this town, so quaint and picturesque that an artist, of a certain type, would be delighted to sketch there.

When we began our descent of Bayou Teche the St. Martinville bridge was opened by the same dapper gentleman—he was a doctor we had learned, substituting as bridge tender for a younger brother who was in the army. The next stop was Keystone Lock, where Happy greeted us and returned our copy of *Kon-Tiki*. After a quick passage downstream to New Iberia, we tied up at our former landing by the sugarhouse above town. The watchman promptly visited us as old friends, and when Anna told him how much we were enjoying his blackstrap, he brought us another canful.

The skiff engine had performed badly on the run up Teche and we determined to trifle no longer but to give it the complete overhaul it should have had when first acquired. A new piston, rings, crankshaft and valves—all Model T Ford parts—were procured from New Orleans overnight by an auto parts company on the highway. The name of the company was Himel, which I thoughtlessly mispronounced—it is "ee-mel" in New Iberia. I tore the engine down, but the installation and adjustment of the new parts were done by an auto mechanic named Mouton and his helper. When it was all put together again the engine could be started only with difficulty and it missed as badly as before.

This was discouraging, to me and to the others who had

concerned themselves with our ailing engine; the first of these being two boys who were working on their own boat in a back yard across the bayou. One of them painted abstractions and showed only a polite interest in my pictures. The boys had taken me to a man in New Iberia who was thoroughly familiar with the old style marine engines. At his suggestion I ground the valves, but this did not help.

As a last hope I began to probe the only old part of the engine which remained—the intake and exhaust manifold, which was a single casting with a separating partition. This partition, I discovered with elation, had rusted through. It was a wonder that the engine ran at all. Now the obliging auto parts company extended their service to get a new manifold from a boat store in New Orleans. When this was bolted in place the engine popped off at the first turn and ran smoothly, then and for the rest of the voyage.

It had been winter when we made the voyage up Bayou Teche. The turn of the season was first noticed when we lay above St. Martinville. In those warm days of late February the grass became green, the wild plum blossomed and a few redbuds showed up among the park trees. Boys began to swim in the bayou, redwings came in numbers, and the *garde-soleil*—sunbonnet in Kentucky—made its appearance.

When we now left New Iberia and continued our downward voyage, March was well along, the shores were bursting with spring. The smell of fresh earth was in the air as Negroes with mules plowed strips of ground along the bayou and planted gardens. We stopped the boat to gather fresh poke, which Anna had spotted from the deck. Wisteria draped over the water, and yards were ablaze with azaleas, camellias and flowers unknown. Blackberries began to bloom, and spider lilies in moist places. Mockingbirds eclipsed the early-singing thrashers, and we saw migrating birds, like the Maryland yellow-throat and white-eyed vireo, which would not reach the shores of the Ohio for six weeks. The cypress put forth tiny fernlike leaves. A most striking change came over the live oaks on which a new growth of yellowish leaves appeared, and the somber foliage of winter was transformed into the fresh green of spring.

On reaching the Charenton Canal, forty-six miles below St. Martinville, we left Bayou Teche and turned southward. For a ways the canal ran through a green forest, then the trees gave way to grass and we were in an open wilderness which extended infinitely far and deep.

IX

The low, almost tideless shores of the Gulf of Mexico are a grassy prairie with many bays and inlets. Often the Intracoastal Waterway is separated from open water by only a narrow verdant strip; enough protection, however, to reassure us as we sailed along, looking out from our decks to a horizon of water.

Now to the west a blue smear appeared above the flat land, like a bluff on the Mississippi River seen from far off. It was indeed high land, Cote Blanche Island, one of the five salt domes of Louisiana. These are not islands in the sea but low, wooded hills rising from the oceanlike land that surrounds them. Cote Blanche is almost a true island because the southern half of it is a rounded point extending into the Gulf, or rather into West Cote Blanche Bay. The Intracoastal skirts the northern side, where we found a slip between the canal and the base of the hill, an excellent harbor for us.

Anna chose to remain on board while I explored the island. Landing at a small dock, I set off with the dogs on a shell road, well-graded but long unused and grass-grown, which sloped upward toward the center of the island. It had been cut through a forest of hardwoods—mostly gum, maple and oak. I saw one magnolia, many dogwoods in bloom, and much poison ivy; few birds, however. It was hill country, and one could hardly believe that he had just left the marsh. The change was as striking as that experienced when climbing from the desert into mountains abounding in green trees and running water.

Cote Blanche dome was about two miles across and I judged the elevation to be less than one hundred feet. No construction or works of any kind could be seen, though no doubt the road, and the slip and dock as well, had been made in an attempt at development. After a ways the road petered out and only dim trails led to the outer shore. This was a sandy beach littered with wreckage and driftwood, some of it good timbers. The length of a rickety, broken pier proved how shallow the water was. Farther to the west the island ended in a clay bluff which may have given rise to the name Cote Blanche. The noble effect of the sea was destroyed, to some extent, by the calm, muddy water and by some oil rigs and tanks which rose from the surface far offshore.

Returning by a different path, I discovered two or three ruined houses not far inland which seemed to be contemporary with the old pier. In their yards lay some unusual iron kettles, eight feet across, gracefully formed, like immense hand basins with flat rims and sloping sides. I guessed they had been used to make syrup or sugar, and played with the idea of taking one with us, as no doubt other people have done; but their size and weight keeps them safe from human pack rats.

Before we could get away from Cote Blanche a wind sprang up from the northwest, and on March 13 it became cold enough to freeze a skim of ice on buckets of water. What must have happened to the gardens on Bayou Teche? The wind was strong for two days, and being offshore it blew so much water out to sea that the level dropped three or four feet. This left our boats stranded in the mud—except the johnboat, which I kept in the water.

We were pleased to remain at Cote Blanche for a few days, knowing that this would be the only island we would see in its natural state. It was a wild forest. The dogs discovered a coon in a hollow tree not far from the boat, and after a battle in which the coon got in some good bites, the unlucky beast was dragged out and killed. The fresh meat was welcome as we had eaten the last of the catfish brought from Bayou Teche.

During these windy days many fishing boats passed, driven from the bays and Gulf into sheltered water. Tug and barge traffic was heavy as usual.

Across the canal was a slip and dock from which machinery and equipment had once been ferried over to the island. A narrow road along a ditch led from the dock north toward inhabited country. We walked a little ways up the road, watching flocks of Louisiana herons, which are dark before and light behind, feeding in the marsh, a snowy egret among them. Grackles squawked from the tall grass, and trim, irridescent tree swallows swooped about. We thought, what a wild place this would seem, at the end of the world, if one had come to the road's end from the interior; yet we were as much at home in this waste land as on Bayou Teche, and more at home than in New Orleans harbor.

By the time we left Cote Blanche the air had lost its sharpness and the water had risen to its normal level. It was an hour's run to Cypremort, a few houses and cane fields on Cypremort Bayou. The poetry of its name, and the scarcity of settlements of any kind along the Intracoastal west of Morgan City, had led us to expect more than was to be found there.

Weeks Island, seven miles to the westward of Cote Blanche, had been in sight all morning, and we felt that we were steering for a real island, though merely plodding along the canal. Weeks Island is a landmark for navigators of the Intracoastal and it makes a fine appearance from the distance with its salt-mine structures and town on the bare hill—a company town with all the houses painted yellow-orange with red roofs. At length we rounded the southern end of the island, passing through a narrow strip of lowland close to Vermilion Bay. Here were docks along the Intracoastal where barges were being loaded and unloaded, and a motley collection of small boats. It was no place for a shantyboat so we went on, and after ducking into a stub canal to be safe from a tow of empties dragging the bank, we entered Weeks Bayou, which circles around the island on the western side.

Relaxing after the morning's run on the busy canal, we tied up to a shell bank where the shore was quite high, all white shells and live oaks. While eating our dinner we were dismayed to see a tug round the sharp bend behind us. It was followed by an empty tank barge, and a second, and a third. We realized at once that we were in a bad spot—on the outside of a curve, with an onshore breeze. We should have known better than to tie up there but it was too late to do anything about it now. The tug was nearly up to us, the end of the last barge was swinging in against the bank. We jumped ashore and waited, tense. The barge looked huge as it rushed toward us, scraping on the shells. It raked the outside of our boat, heeled it way over; there was a crash of breaking timber and the barge passed on.

We quickly inspected the damage. The skiff and johnboat, which were lined up behind the shantyboat, were untouched. The catwalk on the outside of the shantyboat had been torn away, and the pressure of the barge had opened one of the seams a little. This was all. We gave thanks for the three-inch bottom planking; a hull less strongly built might have been crushed.

Meanwhile the tug, which had rounded another bend and tied up its barges, came back to see if we were in distress. After learning that the damage was apparently not serious the captain went on his way, giving us as he departed the tug owner's address in Houston, Texas. We had said little to the captain but in our private opinion he was to blame. Even if we had been in his way he should have made some effort to avoid hitting us, or at least blown a danger signal. Perhaps his idea had been to snap the barges away from the bank by continuing at full speed, but this was impossible with a cross wind blowing.

After this encounter we went up the looping bayou to a road bridge where we were told of outlandish places and bayous farther on—Bayou Gaspergou, Stump Bayou, and Isle de Cane; but since they were too far from Weeks Island we retraced our route and turned into an unpromising branch called Warehouse Bayou, which led to an oil field close to the hill. Several new wells were being drilled, all by floating equipment and machinery, and the narrow bayou was lost in a maze of canals which led to the many wells. It was nearly dark when we found a harbor in a short canal where a well had already been drilled. There it was—a pipe rising from the water with the usual "Christmas tree" of valves and fittings. We let it strictly alone and moored to the bank of spoil which had been dredged out to make the canal.

Our home was in the middle of this oil field for a week and we became used to the clangor of machinery and steel, jets of steam and clouds of smoke, flares, fires, and the smell of oil.

Crew boats passed with workmen on their way to and from the drilling. They must have been curious about our being there and wondered what had attracted a campboat to that unlikely spot.

With this full-scale demonstration going on around us we should have learned something about the drilling of oil wells, but we did not. A change in the sound coming from the nearest of the noisy, grotesque giants might wake us at night, and looking out of the window we could see that section after section of piping was being pulled out of the ground and stood up within the derrick like a bundle of bean poles in a fence corner. On the top platform of the derrick, lighted against the dark sky, men were working, perhaps in wind and rain, with a flimsy protection of flapping canvas. By morning the pipes were all back in the ground and the endless drilling was going on as usual. What it was all about we could only guess.

The slopes and trees of Weeks Island were but a few rods from our boat. One day I walked to the town, two miles away at the other end of the island, following a road through a rolling country of fields and woodland. The town was draped over the bare hill in a loose, haphazard fashion, a rather unnatural place, as company towns are. All the residents have some connection with the salt company and many of them are from the north. There was a general store, very complete and orderly, and a post office which had mail for us. The view over Vermilion Bay to the islands and Gulf beyond was worth coming a long way to see. One could not trust his eyes, the scene was so deceptive and shifting. Those dark islands might be cloud shadows. Was that yellow, muddy water—or marshland? And where did the blue water of the open sea end and the sky begin?

All of us together made another trip to town in the skiff by way of the bayous to the docks on the Intracoastal. We climbed the hill past the cottages, watched a new boat being built in some fisherman's yard, and returning, brought a load of groceries and gasoline down to our skiff.

Frequent showers furnished enough water for a clothes washing. A serious handicap was the lack of trees to tie the line to, but we managed by using the spike-pole and push-pole, and by guying up a long board from the oil well lumber that floated around us. This also supplied me with material to repair the catwalk smashed by the barge.

These chores rounded out our time at this point. On our way out of Weeks Bayou we lost Sambo for several hours after we stopped for breakfast and the dogs went off on a chase. We figured he might have become confused and gone back to our old landing, which was a short way overland, but through a marsh passable only for a dog. I went the long way around in the skiff, and there was Sambo; he seemed to be expecting me.

We now moved far out into the marsh and for the next seven weeks lived in the empty wilderness. Since it was off season for the trappers and hunters, we rarely saw anyone. If our shantyboat life was ever to be monotonous, this was the time and place for it; yet the days continued to be full of interest, and there was so much to do and observe and explore that we could hardly keep up with all of it.

Our first station was in Bayou Carlin, not far from the Intracoastal—the upper works of passing tows could be seen above the tall grass. The low dome of Weeks Island with its water tower lay on the eastern horizon, and if the wind was from that direction it brought us the sound of drilling in the oil field, sometimes so plainly that we could distinguish our former neighbors there, whom we had named the Locomotive and Old Two-beat.

We happened to read at this time *Le Chêne et le Roseau* of La Fontaine. Although the oak was lacking in our scene, we felt close to the reed. Like it, our home was *"Sur les humides bords des royaumes du vent."*

The wind blew unceasingly, from one direction and then another with no pause in between. The south wind was strongest and made us think of hurricanes. It would blow for days at a time, alternating storms and sunshine, building up great mountains of white clouds or tearing them to shreds in a gale. Then the water became salt and rose over the land. If it were not for the tall, thick grass which gave a semblance of dry land to the flooded marsh, we would have been alarmed by the extent of the sea around us.

When the wind veered to the north it brought a sharp, clear air, and if continued for two or three days it blew so much water out to sea that the level dropped a yard or more. As at Cote Blanche, our boat began to beach out, and the decks were aslant until the wind shifted to another quarter and the waters returned.

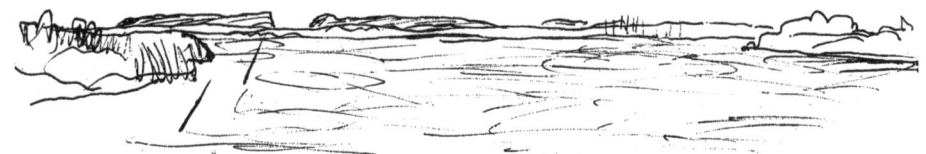

The map of this section close to the Gulf admits that the line of demarcation between fresh and salt water marsh is indefinite. Since the water is too brackish for hyacinths, all the narrow bayous and canals are open to navigation. It was fun to explore them in our skiff. One channel, deep enough for small tugs, led us to New Iberia; it did not connect with Bayou Teche, however. A narrow ditch nearby made a beeline for Weeks Island. We called it the Power Line Canal because of the poles and wires that followed it, and made a trip to town that way.

It was a short run down the bayou to Vermilion Bay. On first sight it looked like the ocean, since no land can be seen to the south. There are some large islands in that direction—bird sanctuaries, as most of the coast is—but they are too far away and too low to be seen from the equally low mainland. The islands break up the ocean waves, and the shores of the bay are as soft and grassy as those along the bayous. We did not venture far out, however, because our skiff rolled too much in the choppy water.

Skipper and Sambo found rabbits to chase in all parts of the marsh. We wondered where the rabbits went when the marsh was under a high tide. At such times I took the dogs to the high shore along the Intracoastal. This was also a source of firewood, often hard to find in the treeless land; and I gathered pokeweed there, too.

One day, after spending a long time digging in the mud, the dogs routed out and killed an animal which in my ignorance I called an otter. The meat looked edible, so we tried it. It was delicious. These animals were quite numerous, and the dogs often wore themselves out by swimming and diving for them. The biggest one we saw, weighing fifteen pounds and almost as large as Skipper, was cornered by the dogs on a mud flat. It put up a stiff fight, the three animals rolling over in the mud, plastering themselves with it until not a hair could be seen. The only bare spots were their eyeballs. After receiving some deep bites, the dogs killed the beast and Sambo dragged it into the grass where I could get hold of it. We ate that one, too.

When we described this animal to some Cajuns later on, they called it a nutria and said it had been brought to this country from South America to be raised in captivity for its fur. In time a few nutrias had escaped into the marsh, where they became wild animals again. Now they are numerous and widespread in Louisiana. The nutria sometimes gets to be twenty-five pounds in weight, and the meat is good to eat, we were told. Our dictionary described it as a marine rat living entirely on plant food. I was not far wrong in calling my first nutria an otter, for the Spaniards did, too; the word means otter in Spanish.

We thought that snakes were less abundant in the marsh than in the wooded country, yet Sambo had his only snake bite at Bayou Carlin. Unlike Skipper, who attacked every snake she saw, Sambo tried to avoid them. He must have stepped on this one by mistake among some bushes along the shore just as he started to swim across to the boat. The poison acted so quickly that I had to help him out of the water. His paw and leg became swollen and livid and the hair came off, but there were no more serious effects.

After three weeks in Bayou Carlin, during which time not a soul came within sight of our boat, we moved a few miles westward via the Intracoastal to another bayou which lay north and south, extending quite a ways inland from the bay. It had been dredged and straightened to make a channel for small tugs and fishing boats, and one of the unused loops of the natural stream afforded a good harbor for us. The boats passing through the channel, bound for the inland port or in the other direction for the Intracoastal or the bay, were pleasant to see, and they made us feel we were part of the world again.

Weeks Island was lost to view. The sound of drilling there did not reach us, nor did the oil-field flares tarnish the splendor of the night. We still had an island to look at, however, for Avery Island lay northeast, distant about two miles.

We had landed near a small dock, and on the shores was a small cabin, hardly more than a shack, which was the winter outpost of some unknown trapper. He had left his pirogue at the dock, tied in such a casual fashion that it made us wonder. The craft was very light, made of thin cypress boards, with sharper ends and more freeboard than the old style pirogues which were hollowed out of a single log. We took turns in trying this one and found it a delight to paddle, so quick and responsive, so well suited to penetrating the narrow grassy waterways. Our own boats were gross and clumsy in comparison.

The cabin, dock, and tangible evidence of human living set this spot apart. Perhaps here was the beginning of a settlement which would have a long history. This feeling of permanence was strengthened by a single tree which stood there, a remarkable object in a land flat and low as water, where one loses his sense of proportion to such a degree that a single bush stands out like an oak, and a hedge of them along a ditch has the appearance of a forest. This particular tree was a live oak, low and scrubby, yet of singular importance because it was the first tree to be seen on coming in from the Gulf. Perhaps it was on account of the tree that this site had been selected for the cabin. The tree had attracted another habitant—a shrike, which was nesting when we were there in April. Here was a genuine pioneer family, living far beyond the frontier, holding the post in the summer while the trapper took over for the winter season.

We enjoyed the company of birds all through the marsh. There were water birds of many kinds—gulls, often the laughing gull, which has a black head, the royal and other terns, cormorant, osprey, killdeer, the black-necked stilt, and many other shore birds. Ducks were common, the blue-winged teal abounding in great flocks. On an expedition to the bay we entered the shallow Tigre Lagoon and saw hundreds of water and shore birds feeding in the mud flats and flying overhead. There were several kinds of herons, and the egrets were everywhere—the American egret with black legs and feet, yellow bill, and the smaller snowy egret with yellow feet. One day a snowy egret sat on our headline fishing, a few yards from us. His egret plumes were plainly visible, extending from head down over back and wings, curving up at the tail.

We were always surprised at the number of land birds to be seen in the marsh. A few bushes were enough to attract the cardinal, towhee, kingbird and others. The grassy marsh was the home of such birds as the rail, bittern and marsh wren, shy and hard to see in the thick, impenetrable grass. We spent much time stalking the wrens. The native long-billed marsh wren was nesting; the short-billed wren, smaller and more warmly colored, was still to be seen, though it is only a winter resident of the marsh.

The short-bill sings in a dry staccato, something like a chipping sparrow; but the native long-bill has a mysterious reedy song, a true voice of the marsh.

At every place we stopped I tried my luck with the cast net, and if a few shad for bait could be caught I set out some bush lines. Sometimes the fishing was so poor that we cooked the shad for the dogs and contented ourselves with a few mullet, if any large enough to eat were taken with the net. At another place and time the catfish might be abundant. I caught one fish we had never seen before. It had a skin the color of a blue cat, with limber spines on the sides and top of the head which were two-thirds as long as the fish. In place of the catfish's whiskers were long white ribbons. The tail was large and forked. This, we learned, was the salt-water catfish, to be eaten only as a last resort; even the dogs did not like it.

No fish of any kind were caught while we lay near the cabin, but soft-shell crabs were abundant. We set out a few bushes and feasted on this delicious food, as did Sambo and Skipper.

After ten days in this quiet harbor we put out with our entire fleet on a cruise of exploration. Our route was northward, inland, over a stream too wide to be called a bayou; hence its name, Petite Anse, Little Bay. After a few miles it divided into three or more narrow bayous. We named this junction Five Points and took the channel to the right, toward Avery Island. The land became a little higher, making a definite bank, and trees appeared. When we pulled in to shore to let a tug and oil barge go by, we discovered some ripe dewberries. The Carolina wren and chat proclaimed the change of terrain.

The bayou was a narrow rift in a jungle of trees and vines. All at once, as if by magic transformation, the right bank became a park with smooth lawns and walks, beds of flowers, blossoming trees, palms and Chinese pagoda. A mingled fragrance came to us, and the songs of wood birds. This was the famous Jungle Gardens of Avery Island. It extended for a mile along the shore, and then the bayou expanded into a small basin. Passing a pile driver at work and some trawlers and motorboats moored to docks, we crossed the basin and found a berth for our shantyboat close to a road. This was the head of navigation; beyond was only a shallow, winding creek, the natural bayou.

After dinner we set out for a walk on the island. There was a toll gate at the beginning, through which the smiling keeper let us pass free; thus it should always be with walkers. Not far within the island was the pond in Jungle Gardens where the egrets nest on platforms of poles and sticks which have been erected for them; hundreds of noisy birds, having laid aside in their homes the elegance and dignity with which they travel abroad. Many of them make expeditions out into the marsh, from which we had often seen them returning at evening in unhurried flight toward Avery Island.

Avery is the highest of the islands, its elevation being 196 feet. It seemed to be an older, longer-settled place than Weeks Island. First its wealth was in cattle, then in the salt mines; today it is in oil. There have been sidelines, like the hot peppers brought in from Mexico and grown here; and the tourist trade, attracted by Jungle Gardens.

We enjoyed our walk along the country road with cottages and a store or two scattered by the wayside. It was two miles to the post office at the south end of the island, where most of the inhabitants live.

If our home had always been in the open marsh, the two days and nights spent at Avery Island dock would have been a harrowing experience. Trucks and cars passed by our windows, even a train, of a few box cars and a passenger coach at the end. There were people about all the time, strangers looking in at us; dust, noise and glaring lights. Yet this was a relatively quiet and countrylike place, a faint suggestion of what a city and highway would be. Surely the "natural man" would not choose to go farther in that direction but would retreat to the quiet, fragrant marsh where all the stars can be seen. The natural habitat of man, however, has become the city, and he is lost and afraid when he is away from its complexity and distractions.

As for ourselves, we were quite at home at the Avery Island dock, where we enjoyed the people and the animation of the scene about us; yet after two days and nights we were happy to get into the green solitude again.

We left Avery Island by a different route and made our way through the network of oil-well canals, marveling at the extent and activity of the oil field and at the barge traffic on such narrow waterways. From a temporary harbor among the oil wells we made another trip to the Avery Island post office, landing our skiff at a dock on a long, straight canal which led to the south end of the island. Then we headed for the marsh, this time to the junction of the bayous which we had named Five Points.

The shantyboat was anchored behind a small island, from which post we could watch the many boats that went by—tugs and barges to and from Avery Island, and trawlers running between the Gulf and their port a few miles farther inland. The southbound fishing boats came directly at us until very close, when they swerved to pass on the other side of the island. One of the tugs attracted our attention by repeated blasts of its whistle. We had been recognized by our friend the *Liberty* from Bayou Lafourche.

Though it was still April we lived on a summer schedule—up early in the cool morning, the big windows of the cabin open all day, meals on the shady deck, and to bed without lamps because of the host of mosquitoes which seemed to rise from the marsh at nightfall. They were not abroad in daylight, and flies did not trouble us ever.

These were unhurried days, when time seemed unlimited as the space about us. There wasn't much to be done—the easy routine of shantyboat life, meals, fishing, a supply of cook wood, which meant a skiff expedition to the woods over toward Avery, berry picking, exploring of new waterways, and sketching. We spent much time out in the sun, poking about with the skiff or johnboat, delighting in the sea breeze, the birds, plants and grasses, while Skipper and Sambo hunted on new shores or played hide-and-seek with nutrias.

The time for reading was extended and our backlog of books proved its value. A hefty volume of American literature seemed inexhaustible, and it took us about as long to read *Arabia Deserta* as it did for Doughty to write the book. No passage in it was too detailed or repetitive. We felt very close to him because the moist wilderness in which we lived was like the desert in many ways, having the same openness, sweep and purity.

Though time meant nothing to us, the days were filled and there was not an idle, aimless minute. We got out our instruments and played nearly every day, often discouraged by our miserable performance, and again soaring to new heights.

My favorite station was on the roof. It was too hot and sunny for Anna, and the dogs could not get up there; so I sat in solitude with pencil, paper and binoculars. The writing I was engaged in was often laid aside in order to make a sketch of the tug or fishing boat that was going by. Such interruptions were frequent because many trawlers passed, sometimes thirty or forty in a day when the offshore waters became too rough for them; and the white boats went out in flocks when the winds moderated.

Or I would cease all work and thought, and just look, sweeping the horizon through every point of the compass. The elevation of the roof raised me above the tallest grass and bushes, and I could see far. Toward the south the grassy marsh faded into the shimmering distance, a vast plain ever changing in color and varied in texture, responsive to the winds that swept above it. The little cabin and tree near our earlier harbor stood out prominently, the only tree and the only geometrical shape in that direction. Some of the watercourses could be traced by their shining surface, others were hidden by tall grass, to be indicated only by a slowly moving boat which seemed to be riding through the marsh. In other directions the flatness was broken by trees and groves, the northern horizon appearing to be a solid forest. Everywhere the landscape was flooded with sunlight or darkened under piled masses of clouds.

We have often wished that we could be like our dogs, perfectly content with the present moment, without foresight or remembrance. It is our lot, however, to be obliged to look ahead, to plan for the future, and in laying out a course, to consider the past as well as the present.

One year in the bayou country of Louisiana had slipped by; a short year, it seemed now, full of novelty and good living. Yet we felt that we did not want to make Louisiana our settled home. The attraction of a more northern air, of hills, gardens, and a known and loved countryside was strong within us. If we were going back to Kentucky, and this we were certain to do in the end, it might be best to leave Louisiana now, before the long, hot summer. In deciding this, we sadly gave up our plans for further exploration to the west; for consolation reminding ourselves that it would be through a marsh country such as this, hundreds of miles of it, and we would have to follow the Intracoastal most of the way, past oil fields, chemical industries, cities and open bays, all of which were not to our liking. We agreed that the country with the greatest appeal was behind us; yet we would have given much to see from our own deck White Lake and Calcasieu, Sabine Pass and Galveston Island.

We decided, then, to move our fleet to Delcambre, the port of the fishing boats, a few miles farther inland; there to dispose of our boats and return to Kentucky overland, as many shanty-boaters and flatboat men had done long before our time.

One sunny afternoon a few days before leaving the marsh we made a last skiff trip, up a narrow, crooked bayou to the west, winding between walls of grass. Here we felt more plainly than ever before the change in the land where it becomes higher, only a few inches perhaps, yet solid and dry enough for trees to grow. We were all at once in a new earth, where leafy branches arching overhead cast shadows, where the grass was clipped by grazing cattle. After a short distance the bank became too high to see over. Landing to look about, we were greeted by half-forgotten sounds and smells—hay, cattle, meadowlarks, rustling leaves. A farmhouse stood nearby and we walked to it, through a gate and around the barn. The house was low and irregular with a long gallery in front. Some men sitting there invited us in and we sat and conversed with the friendly people. Their name was Landry. While Mrs. Landry took Anna into the house—which Anna reported later to be very attractive and well-kept, with modern appliances in the kitchen—I talked with the two Landry brothers who owned the farm. One lived and worked there, the other was Doctor Landry of Abbeville, a town not far off. I asked what crops they raised so close to the marsh. Cattle, hay, rice and corn were mentioned, they had chickens and a large garden, and trapping was a major source of income. I was especially interested in the rice growing. The crop was up a few inches in the fields and ready to be flooded, but the water in the bayous was too brackish. They must wait until an easterly wind brought fresh, muddy water from the Atchafalaya River.

Though farmers, the Landrys had a feeling for boats and for our living on the water. Mrs. Landry showed us an old photograph of a small sailing vessel that had belonged to her grandfather, who was a fisherman. She said they had often sailed out on Vermilion Bay, and to Morgan City, along the coast and up the Atchafalaya.

It was late afternoon when we said goodbye to the Landrys,

with no idea that we would ever see them again, or that they would play an important part in the last chapter of our shanty-boating. Slipping along the narrow stream, homeward bound, making quite a wash on both shores, we soon passed the tree line and entered the marsh, where the earth became moist and instable as if it were about to dissolve. Before this happened, we reached our boat—our home, snug behind the island—just at the moment that the sun, a red ball, dropped below the flat horizon.

X

Delcambre is another of the small Louisiana fishing ports which are not on the coast but inland, in this case ten or twelve miles. The natural bayou on which it is situated has been dredged and straightened to make the Delcambre Canal, a channel for small craft, leading to Vermilion Bay and the Gulf. The canal is also the harbor at the town, where the boats tie up at docks along the shore.

If I were to guess at the number of fishing boats working out of Delcambre, I would say a hundred; there may be considerably more or less. Sometimes the trawlers are lined up two or three abreast, again the docks might be nearly vacant.

On the day of our coming in from the marsh, May 8, about two dozen boats were in port. We did not land in Delcambre but went on by the town, through the pair of bridges and out the narrow canal another mile to a sheet of water called by the fancy name of Lake Peigneur. We stayed a few days by the blue water, happy to be near higher shores and among fields and woods; and we would have remained until our shantyboat was sold had not the location been too unhandy for this purpose. Therefore we returned toward Delcambre and found a mooring for our boat on the east bank of the canal, just short of town.

Here we still enjoyed to some extent the spaciousness of open country. Nothing closed in on us, yet the highway, railroad and the outlying houses of Delcambre were in plain view. After weeks of solitude in the marsh it was exciting to have people and their works to watch, instead of birds and clouds. In time the prospect in every direction became known to us in detail, like pictures in a long-studied book.

The most striking view was to the south, toward Delcambre, in which direction we looked across a small basin of water formed by the widening of the canal. The New Iberia-Abbeville highway ran along the far side of the water and crossed the canal, narrow again, on the silver bridge. Just behind this was the black railroad bridge. Above each rose a steel framework by means of which the bridges were lifted to let boats through. These towers, so close together they seemed one black and white structure, were the highest points for miles around. They dwarfed the tall icehouse by the canal, and were a landmark from every direction in the flat country.

The cottages across the canal, the boats, the buildings along the road, at first a mere pattern of shapes and colors in the landscape, in time came to have a human significance. We felt we knew the people who lived, worked and idled about us, having observed daily their habits and customs. We speculated on the coming and going of our nearest neighbor, Gus, who lived in a campboat. We watched the noon and evening arrival of the man who came home from work in a blue pickup truck. His neighbor walked with a cane, having an artificial foot, the shoe of which remained new and shiny compared with the other on which took all the wear. His wife had a duck and it was claimed that Skipper molested it. A round-faced, smiling Cajun lived near the beer joint at the bridgehead—he kept his smiling countenance even after Sambo had rough-handled his dog. Skipper and Sambo both responded to the stimulation of town life.

After a while even the bridges lost their impersonality. The highway bridge tender came to see us and told about fiddling for local dances. His span was raised and lowered by pressing a button, but that over the railroad was hand-powered. Its keeper

walked round and round a capstan in the center of the bridge, and when he raised it for the night he had to climb down by a ladder. This winding up and down was hard work, and we admired the clever way in which he managed—his system being the result of experience and study—to do the job as few times as possible, and seldom in a hurry. A new man would wear himself out.

A trawler came through the bridge occasionally and turned into the marine ways across the canal basin from us. We watched the work there, the traffic on the road, the daily freight train which came from New Iberia in the morning and back from Abbeville in the afternoon, and many irregular and unexpected trivia through the day, whose hours were marked by the striking of the Delcambre church bell.

Delcambre—or so it impressed us at first—was undistinguished and characterless, a collection of small cottages where fishermen lived, often neat places with gardens. The few small general stores were stocked to meet the wants of the Cajun population at home and afloat. Potatoes and bacon were hard to find, but not rice and cottonseed oil. There was a post office, of course, dependable as they always are, however small.

On our walks to town we usually went around by the docks to see the boats and fishermen, looked in at the net shop, watched quantities of shrimp being unloaded and made ready for processing. Sometimes a trawler would be taking in tons of ice, about to leave for a week's cruise in the Gulf, perhaps as far as the Mexican coast. The boats were of the two or three types standard along the Gulf, most of the newer ones being of the sharp, high-sided model, with pilothouse and cabin forward.

Always about the docks were the pole-and-line fishermen, often women and children, bold as sparrows in a barnyard, ready to drop in a baited hook wherever an opening might be.

As soon as we had settled ourselves in Delcambre, we set about the business of selling our shantyboat, motor skiff, johnboat, gear and equipment—all to one buyer if possible. I felt like a traitor when I tacked a "For Sale" sign on the side of our boat. It was like selling one of our dogs. Yet we were sure of our course and went about it with determination. I put up signs along the road, too, "Campboat For Sale," and told everyone I met.

Meanwhile we reorganized everything on board and did some cleaning and repairing, though not much of this was required as our fleet was always kept in good order, inside and out. The grassy shore at our landing, a yard above the water, dry and open, was excellent for our work. I pitched out a lot of stuff from the roof, the hold and the between-deck section. It looked like a heap of junk but all of it was valuable in our eyes and had served us well. We thought with regret that many of these often-handled pieces, some carried all the way from Brent, must be left behind.

Neither this upheaval nor thoughts of abandoning the boat were allowed to interrupt the even course of our shantyboat life. I put out some trot lines, stretching them from one bank to another, and did much casting. Often a school of mullet came along, churning the water and leaping out to fall back without the grace one would expect of a fish. I might catch several, six or eight inches long, in one cast of the net. They were good to eat and made good cut-bait for catfish.

When town began to seem close we went down the green-shored canal in skiff or johnboat, stopping to pick blackberries and poke, and catching crabs in the lake. Lake Peigneur bordered Jefferson Island, the last island we were to see and the farthest inland. It is the source of Jefferson Island Salt, a brand we had often seen advertised on roadside barns in Kentucky. Knowing it was packed by a Louisville company we had assumed that the name was taken from Jefferson County, in which Louisville is situated. In Delcambre they told us that the salt was named for Jefferson Island where it is mined; and that the island was named for Joseph Jefferson, the famous actor, who once owned it and lived there in a "castle" which still stands. We wanted to visit Jefferson Island but were told that it was not allowed. Thus we missed our last chance to go into a salt mine. It is claimed that the islands are pure salt to a great depth, and the mines are described as a fairy-land of tunnels, pillars and high-arched domes, all white as snow.

Several people from Delcambre came to see the "Campboat For Sale." One was an old man who wanted it for a home. Another, a tall, handsome Frenchman who kept his fishing skiff near our boat, said a friend of his might buy our fleet. I followed up all the local prospects, one being a man I was sorry I could never locate though I went to the house where he was said to live. He was described as "a treasury man," a term which puzzled us until it was explained that he searched for buried treasure, no doubt the lost hoard of Lafitte, the pirate.

Many trappers lived in Delcambre, and we were hoping that one of them would buy our boats to take into the marsh when the season opened. At this time of the year, however, they were not looking for boats and had no money. Only one showed any interest—a young man who in the summer worked in the combination fish-and-liquor store near the bridge. He made us an offer, a low one to begin with, and he hedged on that later, boasting that in the end he would buy us out for next to nothing. When this word got around to us we gave up all thought of selling to him.

Our contacts in this affair and our errands about town gave us a new conception of Delcambre. We began to be conscious of a complexity not at first apparent, and of currents below the surface. A few old buildings, not pretentious but as remarkable when perceived as noble faces in a crowd, proved that Delcambre had deeper roots in the past than flimsy contemporary construction indicated. The place was amazingly provincial, almost foreign, and as self-contained and cut-off as a community in the Kentucky mountains. A large proportion of the inhabitants were of the Delcambre family, if they were not Broussard or Boudreaux. The town was thoroughly Cajun—we heard one person who did not speak French referred to as an American.

Delcambre is pronounced "Del calm," although in New Iberia it is "Dell com." We met many people who spoke only French. A rough-looking but really shy and friendly young man, one of the crew of the trawler *Huley*, came to buy some garden tools I no longer needed. He brought Gus along as interpreter—"Fifty cents, *cinquante centimes*." I did not recognize the words for hoe or rake. Another Cajun was afraid to cross our gangplank because of Sambo growling at the other end. "The dog won't bother you," I said, "speak to him." Knowing that Sambo was not a Cajun dog the man greeted him in his best English, "How-de-do."

We made some good friends here, too. There were the Dooley brothers, for instance, who between them conducted a boat supply store, marine ways and service station, all near the bridge. Jimmy Dooley, whose wit was as sharp as his business sense, was our particular friend and adviser. In spite of his name he was French and was called Doulé by the fishermen; or maybe his name was Doulé, and I misinterpreted it. Jimmy had traveled and worked in the west and this made him more understanding of our situation.

Some of the Delcambre people, unused to strangers, did not know what to make of us. We did not speak their language nor go to their church; we did not drink coffee, and we were not fishermen, though we lived on a campboat. They did not receive us with the friendliness and hospitality shown in other parts of Louisiana. We blamed this suspicious attitude in part on the generally distrustful nature of dwellers in towns compared with country folk, and recalled Doughty's experience in Moslem Arabia, where nomads in the open desert received him kindly, while in town his life was in danger.

During the war the fishermen had been alerted by the Coast Guard and asked to report suspicious craft. In their still unrelaxed vigilance some of them conceived the notion that I was a spy. Did I not ask questions of everyone and write it all down? My sketching from the roof of our boat in the marsh had not been unobserved or forgotten. We were reported to the authorities and investigated by deputies of the parish sheriff, by the state police and town constable. Of course we had plenty of identification, and it took but little common sense to see that we were innocent and harmless.

Common sense, however, is not commonly found. It was no more ridiculous for a Louisiana fisherman to suspect that our shantyboat had been launched from a Russian submarine than for a Lake Michigan Coast Guard officer to think that I was a spy because I sketched the waterfront of a little town. "That's how the Japs got into Pearl Harbor," he had said.

After our honor had been officially established and the natives became more used to us, we lived at Delcambre in peace and enjoyed friendly relations. I was even invited by the keeper of the railroad bridge to be lifted to the top of the tower; he said you could see everything from up there, and I might want to make some sketches.

Since there seemed little chance of finding a buyer for our fleet in Delcambre we enlarged our field of operations. An advertisement in the New Iberia and Abbeville newspapers brought some answers, one being from a man in Lafayette, some twenty miles from New Iberia. I hitch-hiked to New Iberia, rode to Lafayette on a bus, and found the man had an automobile agency. He appeared to be in a bad humor that day, and when I proudly showed him a photograph of our shantyboat—an excellent picture, one of Bernard's—he glanced at it and said, "I might have known you didn't have much for a thousand dollars. What's this stuff on the roof?" It was the bicycle, washtubs, etc., covered with a tarpaulin as neatly as possible.

After this fruitless trip I made an excursion more to my liking on the bicycle. Riding westward a few miles to the town of Erath, I turned south on a dirt road and was soon in marsh country, sniffing the sea wind. I could feel that water was near, everywhere. My first stop was at a country store which was kept by a good-natured German. He must have been something of an artist for he had arranged his stock of canned goods so that the varicolored labels made a fantastic yet regular and repeated pattern across the shelves. This man showed considerable interest in our inland voyage, having as a boy come to that region by water. His entire family had migrated from Virginia, coasting the Gulf shore, there being no Intracoastal Waterway in those days. Near this point their craft was driven ashore in a storm and the father vowed he would not put to sea again. It was not a promising location but this man had prospered, as had his brother, who kept a store some miles to the west.

Receiving several leads here, I pedaled off to see what could be done. My next stop was at the Cycling Plant, an immense layout which resembled a refinery, standing alone in the open country. I approached with some misgivings since it had been hinted by those who considered me a spy that this new cycling plant might be my objective. However, I was cordially received by the head man. He said the sportsmen at the plant would have no use for our campboat because they were building a cabin for themselves in the marsh, but a friend of his in New Iberia—he phoned him at once. Later this friend came to see our boat and we had high hopes, but it came to nothing.

After leaving the Cycling Plant I rode on to the west, stopping at a farm where considerable trapping was done, and at a roadside tavern run by a man who knew all the trappers in the country. I uncovered nothing, but it was a good ride. At length I reached Bayou Vermilion, or Vermilion River, and turned north. The stream was beautiful, winding among the oaks, with picturesque cottages and bridges and small boatyards along its shores. I longed to begin our voyage all over again.

The road led me to Abbeville, a lovely town which did not break the spell of the bayou. After talking with men in a boat store, in a shipyard, and with some fishermen, it occurred to me to call on Doctor Landry, whom we had met with his brother at their marshland farm. It would be a pleasure to see him again, and perhaps he would have some ideas about our problem. To my surprise he said possibly they could use our boat; he would talk it over with his brother.

At this point we let the sale of the boat rest a while and gave our attention to another matter which was urgent. What if we did sell out? We would be left on the bank of the canal with all our personal property, three musical instruments, two dogs, pictures, books, tools and other possessions, some of little value, perhaps, but not to be abandoned for one reason or another. We considered ways and means of getting this stuff back to Kentucky overland, and came to the conclusion that it would be best to buy an old automobile; a decision made with reluctance, for we remembered what a relief it had been to get rid of the car we had once owned. But it seemed the best way out. A car would give us some measure of the independence with which we had traveled by water.

Our first thought was to get a station wagon; then a pickup truck was considered; but these ideas were abandoned in favor of a roomy four-door car with a trailer of some sort for the overflow.

Now we had something to buy as well as something to sell, and no heads for business of any kind. The buying was perhaps the hardest, knowing as little as we did about used cars, and being among strangers with no friends to ask for advice. The first car we considered seriously was a twelve-year-old Buick belonging to a local boy who worked in a New Iberia garage. It was in wonderful condition, with a new motor and red seat covers, but the price asked for it was equal to that of an automobile half the age of this one. We know now that it was not too high, having learned how much can be wrong with an old car, and how much it costs to have the fixing done.

In our perplexity we were visited at the boat one day by a good-natured Cajun with the unlikely name of Ike Romero, who had been tipped off by one of the Dooley boys. Ike's specialty was selling cars to country people, and his easy-going, homely ways inspired confidence. For better or for worse we bought the car he had to offer, a bulging ten-year-old Dodge; in good shape as far as we could see, with a rebuilt motor.

The trailer was easier. In our rambling about New Iberia we had seen a two-wheeled trailer chassis built of steel pipe at a welder's shop. Designed to carry a small boat, it was ten feet long and four wide. I thought I could make something of this and we bought it.

Now on the grassy shore by the shantyboat I began the construction of a body on the trailer frame which would afford cargo space and would unfold into sleeping quarters as well. When completed it was a cypress box ten by four feet, sixteen inches deep, with a light cover made of a pressed wood panel. To unfold, you lifted off the cover, set up a three-foot panel at each end, replaced the cover on top of the panels. Canvas sides were attached and your camp was made. Within was the air-mattress bed ready for sleeping. The bed took up six and a half feet of the ten. In the three-and-a-half-foot end I had contrived shelves and boxes for cooking outfit, food, and all that we considered necessary for comfortable living. The boxes were removable, so that they could be carried to the campfire and used for a table, with our low, folding chairs. Access to the end of the trailer was by side panels, one of which was hinged, making a shelf when opened down. The other panel was loose and could be fastened at the end of the trailer for a work shelf. All this could be done without disturbing the trailer top in case we wanted to prepare a meal, wash, or get at tools and gear without setting up camp. The bed was in a flat tray, removable, and under it was a large storage space.

We were proud of our trailer, built of cypress, varnished, neatly fit to the aluminum-painted frame and wheels. It gave our equipage a unique and individual character, and took the curse off the automobile. We would be able to live along the road as free as gypsies.

It was the middle of June now, and the sun was so hot that I took refuge under a straw hat when working outside. Though we were ready to travel, the boats were still on our hands. It began to look as if we might spend another year in Louisiana, a prospect which we began to anticipate with satisfaction; perhaps we could explore Bayou Vermilion after all.

Then suddenly the outlook changed. Ollie Landry came to the shantyboat one day, and after looking it over carefully, made us an offer, one that was much less than the price we had been asking, but really more than we were expecting to get. It would pay for the car, the trailer and the trip home.

Now began the change-over from boats to land. I made a hard-shell case for the 'cello, which would stand up on the floor of the car inside the rear door, braced against the roof. We had to decide what to leave and what to take. The faithful anchor was abandoned, and also the little cookstove. Anna regretted parting with this, but it was a heavy article to ship and we had no prospect of using it for some time. I promised Anna a new and better stove when we needed one again; still, we both felt there would never be another such lovable stove as this.

On June 28, 1951, after nearly seven years, our shantyboat world came to an end. We lived in chaos for three days—sorting, packing, and shipping what could not be taken with us.

On a fair Sunday morning the last leg of our voyage was made to deliver the boats to their new owner. Missing a favorable tide by waiting for Mr. Landry, we made slow time through the bridges and along the Delcambre docks. After a short run southward we turned into Bayou Tigre, only a boat's length wide and so crooked that someone had to stand on the forward deck to swing the head of the boat around the sharp bends. Reaching the Landry farm we moored the boats to the bank, walked off, and never saw our shantyboat again.

Mrs. Landry invited us to dinner, a feast which was now most welcome. Anna was especially interested in the menu and cooking. There was a roast chicken, which Mrs. Landry served by breaking it into sections with her fingers at the table; rice, and another rice dish with eggplant and meat; the first green corn of the season, fried; also fresh lima beans; preserved figs; no bread, no knives; and coffee of course at the end—drip coffee, the pot kept in hot water, as was the cream.

During the meal our conversation turned to the future of the shantyboat. Mr. Landry's intention was to remove the cabin and make a small barge of the hull, to be used for ferrying cattle and farm implements across the bayous which intersected their land. The prospect had dismayed us, but we consoled ourselves by thinking how preferable this would be to having someone live on the boat in disorder, with no appreciation of the many fine points and intricacies which we had built into it for our own use. And now Mrs. Landry's plans for the boat gave us even more optimism concerning its future. First, she said, they would take a trip in it down the bayou to the islands in the bay where she used to go with her grandfather in his sailboat. Then when the cabin was dismantled she knew just how she was going to use the parts and furnishings. The windows would go into a new addition to their house, which had been a gradual growth from a small beginning. The chests, drawers, cupboards, empty canning jars—all would find their place. We did not know what fate awaited our cherished stove and anchor, but no doubt they would continue their useful existence.

After dinner Mr. Landry showed us about the farm, then drove us to Delcambre, to his mother's house, a gracious old place that gave a new aspect to the town. In midafternoon we were left alone on the canal bank, where no familiar shantyboat welcomed us. All we could do was get into the car and drive off, looking back to see if the trailer was following. Skipper rode between us in the front seat, Sambo had a niche in the back seat which otherwise was piled to the roof. Excited by this new way of traveling, they watched the roadside and barked at every dog they saw.

With the miles our spirits began to rise. After all, we were still together, still shantyboating, on wheels, with all the world before us.

www.ingramcontent.com/pod-product-compliance
Lightning Source LLC
Chambersburg PA
CBHW081419160426
42813CB00087B/2566